sauerbruch hutton

sauerbruch hutton
projekte 1990 - 1996 projects

architecture in the new landscape

Birkhäuser Verlag
Basel · Boston · Berlin

sauerbruch hutton

projekte 1990 -1996 projects

conception/konzept

matthias sauerbruch, louisa hutton

editorial staff/redaktion

vera gloor, ulrike kremeier

translations/übersetzungen

sauerbruch hutton architects

cover design, layout & typeface:

particolare assoziation, gertjan rooijakkers

typeface: sha arqui family

A CIP catalogue record for this book is available from
the Library of Congress, Washington D.C., USA

Deutsche Bibliothek Cataloging-in-Publication Data:
Sauerbruch, Hutton, Projekte 1990-1996;
architecture in the new landscape/
[trans. Engl.- German of the text of Robert
Harbison; Matthias Sauerbruch]. – Basel; Boston;
Berlin: Birkhäuser, 1996
ISBN 3-7643-5348-1 (Basel...)
ISBN 0-8176-5348-1 (Boston)
NE: Sauerbruch, Matthias [Ill.]

© 1996 Birkhäuser – Verlag für Architektur,
P.O. Box 133, CH-4010 Basel, Switzerland
Printed on acid-free paper produced from
chlorine-free pulp. TCF∞
Printed in Germany

ISBN 3-7643-5348-1
ISBN 0-8176-5348-1

9 8 7 6 5 4 3 2 1

robert harbison
sauerbruch hutton in berlin

Berlin ist keine Stadt wie jede andere. Meine erste Ankunft mit dem Zug von München war voller Komplikationen. Ich erinnere mich noch genau an den Schock beim Grenzübergang in die DDR: Endlose Tannen im Schnee, ein unerklärter Aufenthalt und dann die Zone zwischen den beiden Teilen Deutschlands: rasierte Erde, Stacheldraht, futuristische Wachtürme.
Die ostdeutschen Abteile rochen anders und sahen aus wie Züge in Uniform. Nach schmutzigen Dörfern eine triste Industriestadt, Halle, die sich in meiner Erinnerung einprägte, obwohl wir in schier unnatürlicher Geschwindigkeit hindurchrasten: Halle. Es war so seltsam, daß die Menschen auf den Bahnsteigen kaum aufzuschauen schienen, als stünde eine Wand zwischen uns. Ich las viel in diesem Blick: Arbeiter – ausgespuckt, teilnahmslos wartend –, ein unheilbarer Mangel an Frische wie in einem Science Fiction Roman, in dem Schäbigkeit eine grundsätzliche Umwertung aller Werte verbirgt.

Ich habe seither über diesen flüchtigen Kontakt oft nachgedacht, ohne seiner Wirkung gewahr zu sein. Es ist immer eine seltsame Erfahrung, durch einen Bahnhof hindurchzufahren, ohne anzuhalten, aber in diesem Fall war uns das Aussteigen unter keinen Umständen möglich – und sie wiederum konnten nicht einsteigen, so daß wir in gewissem Sinne zu Phantomen wurden.

Wir verbrachten mehr Zeit in West- als in Ost-Berlin, aber einige Bilder aus dem Osten haben sich unauslöschlich eingeprägt – aus der U-Bahn auf einen verlassenen Platz auszusteigen, der sich seit 1945 nicht verändert hat. Schinkels Schauspielhaus – eine Ruine, die beiden Kirchen zu beiden Seiten sogar noch stärker zerstört. Schuttberge in den Straßen, unter denen vergessene Straßenbahnschienen verschwanden. Es war die vollständigste Trostlosigkeit, die ich je gesehen hatte, die rückblickend ungeheuren historischen Wert hatte. Osteuropa wurde für mich gleichsam zum Inbegriff einer Reise durch

die Zeit. In Ost-Berlin schienen wir in die Vergangenheit zurückversetzt zu sein – das Land, in dem die Ideologie totaler Revolution herrschte, war ein Land, in dem sich die Dinge nur sehr wenig bewegt hatten, seit es sich von der Welt absonderte, an die ich gewöhnt war.
Es war schwer, dies nur als Oberfläche zu sehen: Farben, Materialien und veraltete Überbleibsel überbrachten in Ost-Berlin unbeabsichtigt Botschaften über die tiefere Bedeutung dieser Form des Sozialismus.

Zwanzig Jahre nach diesem ersten Besuch scheint es unsinnig, das Verschwinden der DDR zu bedauern, und ich will dieser besonderen Form historischer Nostalgie nicht zur Anerkennung verhelfen. Aber für den Historiker bleiben die Überreste der Vergangenheit interessant – unabhängig von Ihrem Ursprung.
Andere Städte sind bombardiert und wiederaufgebaut worden, aber Berlin ist anders. Sein Zentrum wurde zerstört, und danach wurde über einige der am meisten betroffenen Bereiche eine neue, noch tiefere Wunde gezogen: ein politischer Graben, um die feindlichen Seiten der Nachkriegswelt voneinander zu trennen. Gesellschaftlich war es voller Spannungen, für die Architektur verwirrend. Der interessanteste Aspekt, die Trennlinie selbst, war schwer zu verstehen. Auf ihrer Westseite entdeckte man viel Interessantes, nahm aber immer nur die Hälfte richtig wahr. Verschiedene Faktoren trugen dazu bei, einen von der Betrachtung der Stadt als Ganzes abzuhalten. Orte, die nah beieinander lagen, waren schwer zusammenzubringen, zentrale Bereiche wurden zu Sackgassen, und die Erfahrung, abgeschnitten zu sein, erschien in endloser Gestalt.

Die Frage, die sich für Städte immer erhebt, in welchem Umfang Teile der Vergangenheit überleben dürfen, bekommt in Berlin jetzt neue Dringlichkeit. Das spektakulärste Resultat der Wiedervereinigung war eine Reihe von Baugrundstücken im ehemaligen Niemandsland der Innenstadt, und

hier sind heute die ehrgeizigsten Projekte angesiedelt. Der Bauboom, der jedoch jetzt erst beginnt, wird zum sensationellsten Wiederaufbau einer Stadt im 20. Jahrhundert werden.

Warum fühlt man sich angesichts der bisherigen Ergebnisse so pessimistisch? Aufgrund des ihnen zugrundeliegenden Geschichtsverständnisses. Es mag sich als Illusion erweisen, daß etwas anderes als die rohen Kräfte des Marktes Einfluß haben könnten. "Kritische Rekonstruktion" und andere nachdenklich klingende Beschreibungen dessen, was vorgeht, helfen wahrscheinlich nur als unfreiwillige Beschönigungen, die Ziele der Investoren durchzusetzen.

Unbesehen, ob dies so ist oder nicht – es wird im Augenblick eine beunruhigende historische These ins Feld geführt, die davon ausgeht, daß heutige Architektur das Berlin der Vor-Hitler-Zeit oder gar der Aufklärung wiederbeleben kann, wenn sie sich an den Stadtgrundriß des 18. Jahrhunderts und die Gebäudevolumina des 19. Jahrhunderts hält. So werden bestimmte Regeln heilig, wie zum Beispiel die 22 m Gebäudehöhe – eine Vorschrift die absurd ist, wenn man bedenkt, daß sich gleichzeitig zwei Ladengeschosse unter der Erde befinden (wie z.B. in Teilen der neuen Friedrichstraße). Diese als "beispielhaft" gehandelten Projekte im ehemaligen Ost-Berlin wird man bald als Geschichtsfälschungen erkennen. Es mag beruhigend sein, daß Investoren, Historiker und ein altes preußisches Verlangen nach Ordnung so leicht zur Deckung gebracht werden können, aber es ist eine Vision, die ebenso viel unterdrückt wie sie auferstehen läßt. Unerwünschte Aspekte der Vergangenheit werden ausgelöscht und mit Gewalt vergessen.
Es ist verständlich, daß manche Berliner die vom Krieg hinterlassenen, leeren Räume füllen möchten, nachdem der Zusammenbruch einer Ideologie das Territorium des kalten Krieges freigegeben hat. Aber es ist ein papierenes Verständnis von Stadtgeschichte, auf der Einhaltung aller

Berlin is not just another city. My first entry, by train from Munich, was fraught with menace. The shock of the border crossing into the DDR remains fresh. Lots of fir trees in the snow, an unexplained halt and then the zone between the two Germanys, shaved earth, prison fences and a series of futuristic watch towers.
The East German carriages smelled different, and looked like trains in military dress. After muddy villages, a drab industrial city, Halle, which left a strong impression even though we raced through it at unnatural speed. The strangest thing was that people on the platform didn't really look up, as if there was a wall between us and them. I read a lot into this glimpse: workers disgorged, workers waiting listlessly – a terminal lack of freshness as in some piece of science fiction where shabbiness conceals a great transvaluation of values.

I have thought about this fleeting contact many times since without accounting for its power. Going through a station without stopping is always an odd experience, but this time whatever happened we couldn't get off and they couldn't get on, so that we were both in some way phantoms.

We spent more time in West than in East Berlin but a couple of flashes from the East are most indelibly printed – coming up from the U-Bahn in a deserted square which hadn't changed since 1945. There was Schinkel's Schauspielhaus, a ruin, and the churches which flanked it, even fuller ruins. There were mountains of rubble in the street under which abandoned tram tracks disappeared. It was the most complete desolation I had seen, which assumed in retrospect enormous historical value.
Eastern Europe came to represent a diluted version of such time travel. Being in East Berlin was like being in the past – the land where an ideology of total revolution held sway was a place where things had moved on very little

since it split off from the world I was used to. It was hard to regard this as superficial: colours, textures and antiquated survivals in East Berlin transmitted unintended messages about the deep meaning of this version of socialism.

Twenty years after that first visit it seems perverse to lament the passing of the DDR. I don't think it is a worthwhile enterprise to make this particular historical nostalgia respectable. But for the historian the survival of the past from whatever cause retains an interest.
Other cities have been bombed and rebuilt but Berlin is different. Its centre was flattened and then across some of the most charred flesh was drawn a new and deeper wound, a political crease dividing opposing sides in the post-war world. Socially it was tense, architecturally it was confusing. Its most interesting feature, the dividing line, was hard to observe. If one followed it from the Western side one found many interesting things but got something like half of the story. Various forces cooperated to keep one from seeing the city whole. Places which had been close together became difficult to connect, central areas became cul de sacs and the experience of being cut off appeared in myriad forms.

It is always an issue in cities which part of their past will be allowed to survive and in what quantity. In Berlin now the question is assuming urgent new forms. The most spectacular fruit of the fall of the Wall is a series of building sites in the no man's land which ran through the centre. This is the most ambitious crowd of projects, but the building boom, now in its early stages, will be the most spectacular rebuilding of any city in the twentieth century.

Why does the outcome so far leave one feeling gloomy? Because of the historical vision which propels it. Of course it may be an illusion that anything but crude commercial forces are

having much impact. "Critical reconstruction" and other thoughtful sounding descriptions of what is taking place may be only unintentional window dressing helping to bring developers' goals to pass.

Whether this is so, an alarming historical argument is now mounted which holds that present day architects can recover a pre-Hitler, even an Enlightenment Berlin by observing eighteenth-century street patterns and nineteenth-century massing. So certain consistencies become sacred, like a twenty-two metre building height, strictness which becomes absurd when one notices that there are two floors of shopping below ground. These are the conditions which obtain in the rebuilt Friedrichstrasse, a showcase project almost entirely in the old East Berlin which will be recognized before long as a historical fake.
It may be soothing to think that developers, historians and an old Prussian craving for order can converge so conveniently, but it is a vision which suppresses as much as it resurrects. Unwanted regions of the past will be blotted out and forcibly forgotten.
It is understandable that some Berliners want to fill in all the empty spaces left by the war, now that the collapse of one ideology has freed territory formerly tied up in the confrontation. But it is an unimaginative view of the history of cities to set about observing all the old boundaries, as they did in London, frustrating Wren, after the Great Fire.

There was a chance for Berlin to be a new kind of city, of looser texture, not a garden city or imitator of that genre but a city that remembered the past in some of the holes and breaks that violence had created. It does violence to history to pretend that Berlin can be just another metropolis, as healthy and complete as any other. This, an outsider thinks, evades some painful truths, which is not a plea for un-

alten Baulinien bestehen zu wollen, wie es zum Beispiel in London – zur Frustration Wrens – nach dem großen Feuer geschah.

Berlin hatte die Chance, eine andere Stadt zu werden, eine offenere Struktur, keine Gartenstadt oder ähnliches, sondern eine Stadt, die sich an die Vergangenheit in Form von einigen ihrer gewaltsam entstandenen Lücken und Brüchen erinnert. Zu behaupten, daß Berlin intakt und vollständig sein könnte wie jede andere Großstadt, würde die Geschichte vergewaltigen. Man würde – zumindest von außen betrachtet – einigen schmerzhaften Tatsachen aus dem Wege gehen; was nicht als Plädoyer für eine endlose Schuld verstanden werden sollte, sondern für einen Baumeister wie Carlo Scarpa, der uns zeigen würde, wie man sich in seinen eigenen Ruinen wohl fühlen kann.

Berlin braucht eher einen Carlo Scarpa als einen Jean Nouvel oder einen I.M. Pei (um nur zwei der interessantesten Außenseiter zu nennen, die eingeladen wurden). Gibt es den Carlo Scarpa bereits, den Berlin braucht – ohne daß von ihm viel Gebrauch gemacht würde – in der Form eines deutsch-englischen Hybrids, dem jungen Büro sauerbruch hutton? Es scheint nicht der naheliegendste Vergleich, da sie viel kompromißlosere Modernisten sind als er, aber bis zu einem gewissen Grad scheint er angebracht wegen ihres besonderen Interesses am Ort, ihrer Sympathie für die Vielfältigkeit und ihrer Gabe das, was viele als zutiefst negative Eigenschaften der Stadt betrachten, zum Positiven zu wenden.

Der Hang, die hartnäckigsten Probleme einer Stadt anzugehen, läßt sich in Matthias Sauerbruchs Arbeit recht weit zurück verfolgen. Vor ungefähr 12 Jahren gab er seinen Studenten an der Architectural Association Entwurfsprojekte in Birmingham's Bull Ring und den dazugehörigen Stadtautobahn-Brücken. Ich fand diese Orte so abstoßend, daß ich jede Reaktion außer der Flucht nicht verstehen konnte. Viele Projekte im vorliegenden Buch sind Weiterentwicklungen von Gedanken entlang jener Linien, die durch die lautesten, und rauhsten Teile von Birmingham liefen.

Es gibt sicher Architekten, die einfach vom Geld angezogen werden, das in Berlin im Augenblick fürs Bauen ausgegeben wird und soviele Möglichkeiten bietet. Matthias Sauerbruch und Louisa Hutton sind natürlich auch an der Chance interessiert, zu bauen, aber Berlin entspricht auch ihrem eigensten Anliegen, das Leben in den Städten zu intensivieren und sie bewohnbarer zu machen.

Die vorgestellten zehn Projekte stehen für die nicht nachlassende Bemühung, über die Natur der Stadt und ihre Möglichkeiten nachzudenken. sauerbruch hutton beginnen mit einer offenen und toleranten Einschätzung der Arbeit vergangener Stadtbaumeister, mit der Suche nach Schönheit in den verschmähten und ungeliebten Aspekten der Vergangenheit, wie zum Beispiel ostdeutschen Wohnungsbauprojekten aus den Fünfzigern und Siebzigern, die für andere nur eine Ideologie verkörpern. Ein sehr gutes Beispiel ist ihre Akzeptanz des großen Maßstabs der Hochhäuser an der Leipziger Straße, ein Boulevard, der im Augenblick zurückgebaut wird, um eine fixe Vorstellung von "Straße" zu verwirklichen. (Der "Boulevard" ist im Augenblick ein nicht denkbarer Gedanke.) sauerbruch hutton scheinen fähig, bestehende Situationen zu erkennen, die beinahe funktionieren und deshalb nur Verstärkung oder Anpassung brauchen, um positiv zu wirken. Zu dieser Kategorie gehört eine Promenade zwischen alternden Wohnblocks in Marzahn.

In der kurzen Zeit seit der Wiedervereinigung haben sie sich im Rahmen offener und eingeladener Wettbewerbe mit einer erstaunlichen Vielfalt von Problemen auseinandergesetzt. Sie reichen von der Neuplanung eines Stadtteils bis hin zum Entwurf einer Grundschule. Sie umfassen den Umbau bestehender Komplexe, die Regeneration von Industriebrachen und den Entwurf von Staatsgebäuden in der unmittelbaren Nähe wichtiger Bauten aus dem 18. und 19. Jahrhundert, Schloß Bellevue und dem Reichstag. Allen Eingriffen ist eine undoktrinäre Herangehensweise gemeinsam und die Resultate sind normalerweise unauffällig, die Konzepte radikaler als sie aussehen. Das mag in einigen Fällen weniger stark zutreffen und vielleicht wird man seine Meinung ändern, wenn das erste große Gebäude – die Hauptverwaltung der GSW, die jetzt gebaut wird – fertiggestellt ist.

Das Grundstück der GSW gehört zu den toten Ecken, die plötzlich mitten in der Stadt lagen, als die Mauer fiel. Der Kern des Projektes ist ein bestehendes Hochhaus aus den fünfziger Jahren, ein Stück Nachkriegs-Optimismus, dessen Wertschätzung ohne sauerbruch hutton wohl ausbliebe. Es hat ein außenliegendes Traggerüst, das wie ein Eisenman-Konzept-Raster aussieht, im Augenblick aber mit unansehnlichen Asbest-Paneelen verkleidet ist. Der kühnste Teil ihres Vorschlags besteht in der Akzeptanz (anstatt der Verdrängung) dieses Hochhauses, indem ein höheres, leicht gekurvtes Glasgebäude angeschlossen wird. An seiner Basis – dem Gebäude der Vereinten Nationen in New York vergleichbar – liegt ein fülliges "Ei" auf einem kontrastierenden, horizontalen Block mit öffentlichen Nutzungen wie z.B. einem Cafe, das den Platz und die Wege um das Hauptgebäude beleben wird. Der Grund, weswegen meiner Ansicht nach das Gebäude am Ende aufregender sein wird als jegliche Darstellung zeigt, ist, daß es in einer seltsamen Art und Weise farbig sein wird, eine große Masse, geheimnisvoll transparent, mehr wie ein komplexes Lebewesen als eine hartkantige Scheibe. Dies war das erste in einer Reihe von Projekten, die sonst ungeliebte Teile der Stadt in ein neues Gesamtensemble einschließen, ohne sie ihres Charakters zu berauben. Das nächste war ein Projekt für die Heinrich Heine Straße, das einen von der Mauer zerteilten Raum wieder zusam-

ending guilt but for a builder like Carlo Scarpa who would show one how to be at home in one's ruins.

Berlin needs a Carlo Scarpa more than it needs a Jean Nouvel or an I.M. Pei (to mention two of the most interesting outsiders who have been invited in). Is the Carlo Scarpa Berlin needs already there, but virtually unused, in the form of a German-English hybrid, the young practice sauerbruch hutton? It is not the most obvious comparison, for they are much more uncompromising modernists than he. But perhaps a residue of aptness lies in their alertness to site, their sympathy with many sides of Berlin and their ability to turn what others see as deeply negative urban facts into positives.

The penchant for tackling the most intractable urban problems runs quite far back in Matthias Sauerbruch's practice. About twelve years ago he was setting his students at the Architectural Association projects in the Bull Ring and associated urban fly-overs in Birmingham. These were sites I found so repulsive I couldn't understand any response but flight. Many of the projects in the present book are further thoughts along the same trajectory which passed through the noisiest, most riven parts of Birmingham.

There must be architects who are drawn to Berlin simply by the money being spent on building there, which creates so many opportunities. sauerbruch hutton are of course drawn by the possibility of getting things built, but also by a longstanding concern with making cities habitable, and the life in them more intense.

These ten projects represent a sustained effort to think about what a city is and can be. sauerbruch hutton begin from a wide and tolerant appreciation of the efforts of past city builders, finding beauties in the most despised or unfashionable moments of the past, such as East German housing of the 1950's or 1970's, in which others see only alien ideology. A stunning example is their appreciation of the grand scale of the blocks flanking Leipziger Strasse, a boulevard currently being narrowed in the service of a certain notion of the Street (the Boulevard being currently an unthinkable thought).

sauerbruch hutton also seem adept at identifying features of existing situations which almost work, and therefore only need reinforcing or adjustment to become positive. In this class is the promenade between the ageing blocks of Marzahn.

In the short time since the Wall came down they have tackled a striking variety of sites in Berlin, most of them in open or invited competitions. These projects range in scale from the replanning of districts to the design of a small school. They include rehabilitation of existing complexes, repopulating of industrial wasteland and the design of ceremonial premises in close proximity to major eighteenth and nineteenth century monuments, Schloss Bellevue and the Reichstag. All are characterized by an undoctrinaire approach and the results are generally undemonstrative, the thinking more radical than it is allowed to look. Perhaps this is less true in some cases than others, and perhaps when their first large project, the GSW headquarters now under construction, is complete there will be reason to revise this view.

The GSW site is one of those dead-ends which when the Wall came down was suddenly central. The core of the project is an existing 1950's skyscraper, a piece of period optimism which it takes sauerbruch hutton to make one appreciate. It has an externalized structural frame, which looks like an Eisenman conceptual grid, now covered in clumsy asbestos panels. The boldest stroke in their proposal is to embrace the high-rise rather than disowning it, by attaching a higher, lighter, curved glass to it.

At the base, somewhat on the principle of the UN in New York, is laid a plump egg on a contrasting horizontal block which will contain public spaces such as a café which animates the plaza and passages around the main block. The reason I think the building may finally be more exciting than any representation conveys is that it will be strangely colourful, the largest mass mysteriously transparent, so the total result may be more like a complex creature than another hard-edged slab.

This was the first of a number of projects which adopt a generally unloved part of the city and incorporate it without denaturating into a new whole. The next was a site on Heinrich Heine Strasse, knitting up the spatial wound left by the Wall. Here they freed green spaces from cars in one part while increasing the density in another to make a new kind of street. The geometry of this layout with its slightly canted lines is odd enough to create some arresting spaces.

This design could almost be regarded as training for their most ambitious venture of this type so far, a proposal for reviving the largest socialist housing project of the 1970's at Marzahn near the northeastern perimeter of East Berlin, on the urban outskirts.

This is politically sensitive terrain. Apparently there is a strong desire in some quarters to erase the socialist traces, violating the original conception deliberately to show its bankruptcy. This is not the sauerbruch hutton approach. The present pattern of the site consists of a file of towerblocks and slabs. The pattern isn't stultifyingly regular but doesn't make quite enough sense, certainly not when one becomes a pedestrian.

Unlike other entrants in this competition sauerbruch hutton's main effort was to find a logic in the towers and create a public space bridging the hollow between them and the low blocks nearby. The principal means for creating this continuity and life is a low twisting block they call the snake which weaves down the space between, filled irregularly with shops and public services which culminates in an ovoid depart-

menfügt. Hier wurden einerseits Autos aus Grün-räumen entfernt, andererseits Bereiche verdich-tet, um eine neue Art von Straße herzustellen.
Die Geometrie dieses Stadtgrundrisses mit seinen leicht schrägen Linien ist so außergewöhnlich, daß einige atemberaubende Räume entstehen würden. Diesen Entwurf könnte man beinahe als Vorbereitung für ihr ehrgeizigstes Projekt dieser Art betrachten, nämlich den Vorschlag für die Wiederbelebung des größten sozialistischen Wohnquartiers der siebziger Jahre in Marzahn an der nordöstlichen Peripherie Ost-Berlins. Dies ist politisch empfindliches Terrain, denn anscheinend besteht bei manchen der starke Wunsch, die Spuren des Sozialismus auszuradieren und dessen Zusammenbruch mit der bewußten (Zer-) Störung seiner Grundkonzepte zu demonstrieren. Anders bei sauerbruch hutton: Die vorhandene Struktur dieses Ortes besteht aus einer Reihe von Wohnhochhäusern und -scheiben. Ihr Rhythmus ist nicht von nervtötender Regelmäßigkeit, macht aber auch keinen richtigen Sinn, insbesondere wenn man sich zu Fuß bewegt.

Im Gegensatz zu den anderen Teilnehmern an diesem Wettbewerb bemühten sich sauerbruch hutton in erster Linie darum, räumliche Logik im Bestand zu finden und öffentlichen Raum zu ent-werfen, der die Hochhäuser mit den niedrigeren Zeilen gegenüber verbinden würde. Das Haupt-element zur Herstellung dieses Kontinuums nen-nen sie eine "Schlange", die sich durch den Raum windet, unregelmäßig mit Läden und öffentlichen Einrichtungen bestückt und in einem ovalen Kauf-haus gipfelnd, in dem Fußgängerrouten, Parkhaus und Einkaufsetagen unzertrennlich miteinander verschlungen sind.
Dieser – vielleicht idealistische – Gebäudeentwurf ist ein Emblem für die Ziele des Projektes, Funk-tionen und Bewegungsarten nicht voneinander zu trennen, sondern sie miteinander zu verbinden, ja sie zu vermischen. Es bringt den toleranten Städte-bau der Architekten sehr deutlich zum Ausdruck – obwohl ich fast vermute, daß die Autofahrer mehr

Spaß dabei hätten als die Fußgänger.
Man könnte dies als den Entwurf mit den offen-kundigsten sozialen Ambitionen betrachten, der sich mit Fragen von Arbeit und Freizeit, Handel und Mobilität auseinandersetzt, der präzise, aber flexible Antworten auf eine der großen städte-baulichen Fragen des zwanzigsten Jahrhunderts anbietet: die Rolle des Autos in der Stadt. Die Überleitung dieser flächenhaften Vernetzung von Themen zu einem "Regierungsgebäude im Park" scheint auf den ersten Blick ein Rückzug zu for-malistischen Spielen. Aber für kompromißlose Modernisten enthält ein Projekt wie das neue Bundespräsidialamt neben dem Schloß Bellevue aus dem 18. Jahrhundert mitten im Tiergarten besondere Herausforderungen. Um die Probleme ungefähr verstehen zu können, muß man sich einen Entwurf für ein Bürogebäude neben Ken-wood House im Hampstead Heath vorstellen. An-scheinend versteckten die meisten Wettbewerbs-teilnehmer ihre Gebäude in den Bäumen und nahmen damit große Teile des wertvollen Park-geländes in Anspruch.

Die sauerbruch hutton Lösung ist kompromiß-loser und eleganter: ein purer, transparenter Kör-per, der – wie das Schloß – direkt an einer großen Straße durch den Park liegt.
Barock und Rokoko sind mitunter die schwierig-sten historischen Momente für die Moderne. Ihre Fröhlichkeit und Leichtigkeit und ihre Irrationalität wurzeln in einer sozialen Konstellation, die nicht weiter von der Moderne entfernt sein könnte. Andererseits gab es auch Modernisten, denen an Eleganz lag und die sich nicht vor luxuriösen Materialien fürchteten, Mies in Barcelona bei-spielsweise oder Mies in der Interpretation des jungen Philip Johnson in seinem eigenen Haus.

Das erwähnte Projekt ist jedoch kein Pavillon oder Lusthäuschen mit relativ präzisen Vorbildern im Rokoko, sondern ein normaler Verwaltungsbau für die Büros des immer größer werdenden Teams eines Top Managers.

Es mag schwerer gefallen sein, als man denkt, aber der Entwurf scheint genau richtig. Er ist denkbar einfach – eine gutplazierte und wohl-proportionierte Glaskiste. Bei genauerer Betrach-tung erkennt man ein Gebäude im Gebäude, und – zur Seite – eine Glashalle. Es zeigt Mut und Selbstvertrauen, eine solch klare und schmuck-lose Idee in einem solchen Kontext vorzuschla-gen, der zu Gesten, gar Übertreibung einlädt. Wie Mies glauben diese Architekten, daß die richtige Antwort auf eine große Aufgabe manchmal die einfachste sein kann, beinahe nur eine Silbe.

Der Entwurf für die Büros der Abgeordneten des deutschen Bundestags gegenüber dem Reichstag ist diesem Projekt verwandt, aber größer und komplexer. Hier werden im Grundriß Masse und Raum, (private / besondere mit öffentlichen / allgemeinen Räumen) – wie ein dreidimensionaler Mondrian – mit einem komplexen spiralförmigen Erschließungssystem ineinandergewoben. Die Außenseite hat den Effekt einer minimalistischen Skulptur, die die Komplexität des Innenlebens verbirgt. Die sich abwechselnden Bänder der Fassade dienen als Sonnenschutz, Tagesbelich-tung und der Belüftung, so daß die beabsichtigte Zweideutigkeit in Materialität und Proportion ihre Begründung in diesen Funktionen erhält.
Der Entwurf besteht aus sich durchdringenden Elementen. So wie ein Maler mit einer Farbe alle anderen Farben eines Bildes ändert, verursachen hier Änderungen in der Technologie des Gebäudes Änderungen in der Fassade und in der geometri-schen Organisation.
Was auch immer es sei, das zuerst ihre Entwürfe bestimmt – sicherlich nicht die Außenansicht. Folglich ist die Ästhetik ihrer Gebäude schwer zu klassifizieren, obwohl die Verbindung zur puren oder essentiellen Moderne einen roten Faden bietet.

Ich respektiere ihre Arbeit am meisten wegen ihres Ernstes im Umgang mit der Stadt. Dies ist Architektur als Disziplin weitreichender Intelli-

ment store where pedestrian ramps, car parking and shopping floors are inextricably united. This – perhaps idealistic – feature could stand as an emblem of the aims of this project, not to separate but to join and even confuse functions and modes of transport. It expresses the architects' tolerant urbanism at its most expansive, though I continue to think it would be more entertaining for the cars than the other participants.

We might regard this as design with the most obvious social mission, grappling with questions of work, leisure, commerce and mobility, meeting head-on yet flexibly one of the great planning issues of the twentieth century, the place of cars in urban space. To move from this matted tangle of issues to ceremonial buildings on parkland sites may seem at first like a retreat to safety or at least to formalist games. But for uncompromised modernists there are special challenges in projects like new offices for the Federal President near the eighteenth century Schloss Bellevue in the Tiergarten, central Berlin's largest park. Suppose that it were necessary to put an office block next to Kenwood on Hampstead Heath and one has some idea of the issues involved. Apparently other entrants in this competition generally hid their proposals in the trees, thereby eating away at this scarce parkland.

The sauerbruch hutton solution is more uncompromising and elegant, a pure, transparent rectangular block which like the eighteenth century Schloss sits squarely along the axial road through the park.

Baroque and Rococo are amongst the most difficult historical moments for modernism to relate to. Their gaiety, lightness and hints of irrationality have their roots in a social provenance as far from modernism as possible.

But of course there have been modernists who valued elegance and were not afraid of luxurious materials, Mies in Barcelona or, better

yet, Mies as filtered by Philip Johnson in his own house.

Still, the present project is not a pleasure pavilion or personal hideaway, briefs which have fairly precise antecedents in the Rococo. Instead, this brief is looking to fill some dull administrative requirements, providing office space for an executive's burgeoning staff.

I don't know how difficult it was to achieve but their design is one of those which feels exactly right. It is exceedingly simple, a beautifully placed and proportioned glass box. When one comes nearer it is revealed that there is a building within the building, a glazed internal court placed off centre. It shows great nerve and confidence to propound such a clear and unadorned idea in such a context, a context which seems hospitable to elaboration, even to various forms of excess. Like Mies, these architects believe that the right response to a grand opportunity may sometimes be the simplest imaginable, almost a monosyllable.

Near kin to this project though larger and more complex is the proposal for a legislative office building near the Reichstag, which in plan is a locking together of solid and void (private, specific vs. public, general spaces) like a three-dimensional Mondrian which incorporates complex spiral circulation. Here the exterior treatment produces an effect like minimalist sculpture, concealing what takes place within. There are alternating bands of louvres which protect from the sun or let in light or air, so the indeterminate shimmer has its justification after all in the living conditions it produces.

It is a design of interlocking parts: like a painter who, changing one colour, changes those around it, here changes in the technology provoke changes in cladding material and geometrical organization. Whichever comes first in the design, it is not external appearance and thus their buildings are very hard to type visually, though obviously the relation to pure or

essential modernism remains a kind of thread.

I value their practice most for the seriousness of their encounter with the city. This is architecture as a large species of thought, intellectually alert and socially responsible. But personally I like best a couple of smaller, softer projects, the Jewish School of 1990 and the Photonics Centre of 1995 the most interesting bit of which will be built. These projects share indeterminate or irregular overall shape; they are blobs rather than rectangles. Perhaps this is a misleading resemblance for it arises from different causes on the two sites, one of which is a patch of woodland in the city while the other is a semi-desolate industrial landscape on the edge of a disused airfield.

The school gets its aqueous form so that it can melt into its surroundings, the research building so that it will contrast with the rectilinear forms around it. But even here not so that it can engage in competition but to weave its way among a crowd which is inflexible enough already: the new organic forms will mitigate the prevailing asperities.

It would be totally out of character for sauerbruch hutton to personify their little school building in talking about it. This is not the way they think, and they might regard it as foolish, even dangerous delusion. But they do talk about tents and caves, the most primitive types of shelter, in connection with this project. Like Scharoun and other serious designers of schools perhaps here they have let themselves go, thinking broadly about childhood and growth. The result is a design more indeterminate and less formally bounded, which enacts growth in irregular meetings with the world outside and in bringing light down deep into the interior in the pools they call vases (a term which views them in section rather than plan).

genz – intellektuell und sozial verantwortlich. Persönlich mag ich jedoch die kleineren, "weicheren" Projekte am liebsten: die Jüdische Schule von 1990 und das Photonikzentrum von 1995, dessen interessantester Teil jetzt gebaut werden wird. Diesen Projekten sind unbestimmte oder unregelmäßige Gesamtformen gemeinsam: sie sind "blobs", keine Rechtecke. Möglicherweise ist die Ähnlichkeit irreführend, denn sie ist aus verschiedenen Gründen an beiden Orten entstanden – einer davon ein Waldstück, der andere am Rand eines brachliegenden ehemaligen Flugplatzes. Die Schule hat ihre flüssige Gestalt, um in ihrer Umgebung aufzugehen, das Laborgebäude wegen des Kontrastes mit den es umgebenden Rechteckformen; aber selbst hier nicht in der Absicht zu konkurrieren, sondern um sich in eine Gruppe einzuflechten, die ohnehin schon starr genug ist. Die neuen organischen Formen werden die dominante Strenge abmildern.
Es wäre untypisch für sauerbruch hutton, ihre kleine Schule mit Worten zu beschreiben. Sie würden das vielleicht als naive, gar gefährliche Täuschung betrachten. Aber sie sprechen im Zusammenhang mit diesem Projekt von Zelten und Höhlen, den primitivsten Behausungen. Wie Scharoun und andere, die ernsthaft über Schulgebäude nachgedacht haben, haben sie hier Assoziationen von Kindheit und Wachstum freien Lauf gelassen. Das Resultat ist ein eher offener Entwurf, formal weniger eingegrenzt, der Wachstum in unregelmäßige Begegnungen mit der Außenwelt darstellt; Licht wird tief in Räume im Inneren hinuntergeführt, die sie "Vasen" nennen (ein Begriff der eher aus dem Schnitt als dem Grundriß abgeleitet ist).

Das letzte Projekt – das Photonikzentrum – hat, wie immer, interessante städtebauliche Intentionen, aber ich möchte auch seine malerischen Aspekte hervorheben. Die farbigen, transparenten Paneele seiner Fassade demonstrieren nach innen wie außen optische Prinzipien und stellen zugleich eine beinahe vollständige Vereinigung von Malerei und Architektur dar. Le Corbusier brachte in seinem Spätwerk seine Architektur seiner Malerei näher, zuvor hatte er sie als separate Disziplinen betrachtet von denen er behauptete, daß sie gleich wichtig seien.

Wie sauerbruch hutton in ihrem Londoner Haus Farbe als ein plastisch/räumliches Medium benutzen, gibt einen wunderbaren Vorgeschmack auf das, was aus ihrer dreidimensionalen Malerei werden könnte. In diesem Raum an der Spitze eines Londoner Hauses wird man von sechs starken Farben von den eigentlichen Raumgrenzen befreit: Nahes scheint entfernter oder näher, Maßstab und Distanz verschwimmen. Wände, die beinahe vollkommen mit Schränken bedeckt und mit einer starken Farbidentität versehen sind, werden zu riesigen Möbelstücken. Es ist so einfach und so konzeptuell wie ein abstraktes Bild, aber es erreicht eine wundersame Veränderung eines tatsächlichen Raumes. Es wird zu einer deutlichen Demonstration, wie Architektur, den Raum, den sie gebaut hat, wieder auflösen kann und uns von seinen physischen Grenzen befreit. Diese stark farbigen Wände bewegen sich nicht; aber sie suggerieren Bewegung und bereichern unser Gefühl für die Möglichkeiten des Lebens.

The last project, the photonics centre, has, as always, interesting intentions toward urban space, but I want to single out its painterly aspects. Inside and out, the coloured translucent panels in which it is covered give scientific demonstrations of optical principles and are at the same time a near union between painting and architecture. At a certain stage late in his career Le Corbusier brought his architecture nearer to his painting which had earlier been a separate line he pretended to consider equally significant.

In their London house sauerbruch hutton's use of colour as a moulder of space gives a wonderful taste of what this three dimensional painting might turn into. In this room at the top of a London terrace house, six strong colours liberate one from the actual boundaries, making near seem far or nearer, playing tricks with distances and sizes.

Walls become giant pieces of furniture by being coated almost entirely with cupboards and given a strong colour-identity. It is as simple and as cerebral as an abstract painting, yet it achieves a magical transformation of an actual space. It forms a clear demonstration of how architecture can take a space apart which it has made, freeing us from literal constraints. These intensely hued walls do not move but suggest movement and thus increase our sense of life's possibilities.

architecture in the new landscape

Dieses Buch enthält 10 Projekte für das wiedervereinte Berlin, die von sauerbruch hutton während der ersten Hälfte der 90er Jahre entworfen wurden. Jedes Projekt ist eine Fallstudie für einen bestimmten Ort und die damit verbundenen programmatischen Anforderungen, die die Verschiedenheit und Individualität von Architekturen im späten 20. Jahrhundert wiederspiegelt.

This book contains 10 projects for the reunited Berlin undertaken by sauerbruch hutton during the first half of the 1990's. Each project is its own case study dealing with its own particular site and particular programme reflecting the diversity and specificity of architecture in an urban environment of the late 20th century.

Versucht man den Begriff "Landschaft" jenseits seiner offensichtlichen Bedeutung zu definieren, mag man zunächst Horizontalität assoziieren, den Horizont, den Himmel. Man mag an die Existenz verschiedener natürlicher Phänomene wie zum Beispiel Felsen, Wälder, Wiesen, Wasser und einzelne Bäume und Pflanzen denken, die durch nichts als durch die Regeln ihrer eigenen Existenz miteinander verbunden sind.

When trying to define "landscape" beyond its meaning of a recognizable area of countryside one may associate firstly horizontality – openness – the sky. One may be thinking of the loose coexistence of a variety of phenomena such as rock formations, forests, meadows, water and individual trees and plants which are unified into one by no particular order other than the rules of their own existence.

Der Begriff wird jedoch auch benutzt, um künstliche Welten zu beschreiben: Stadtlandschaft, Bürolandschaft usw. sind feste Bestandteile unseres täglichen Wortschatzes.

"Landschaft" steht für Systeme, die keiner offensichtlichen Hierarchie folgen, in der das Einzelelement Bestandteil und Ursache des Ganzen ist. Landschaft suggeriert formale Komplexität im Überfluß, Fluxus von Form und Hintergrund.

The reunification has cast Berlin into a significant rôle. The size and importance of its "re-foundation" after its 45 years of division makes it by default a "pioneer of the future". Designing in Berlin in the 1990's requires an attitude towards the future of architecture in the European city.

In Träumen steht (nach C.G.Jung) die Landschaft für das Ungewisse, in unserer bewußten Symbolsprache werden Landschaften eher mit der Vorstellung individueller Freiheit verbunden – was Landschaftsbilder zu einem bevorzugten Klischee der Werbung werden ließ.

However, the term is also used to describe artificial environments. Cityscape, urban landscape, office landscape etc. are phrases which have entered our everyday vocabulary.

Landschaft ist mit Lebendigem assoziiert, Landschaft impliziert Wachstum und Verfall, den Kreislauf des Tages und der Jahreszeiten ...immerwährende Veränderung.

Die Wiedervereinigung hat Berlin unvermittelt ins Rampenlicht gestoßen. Der Umfang und die Bedeutung der "Wiedergründung" Berlins nach der 45jährigen Trennung macht es automatisch zum "Pionier der Zukunft". Um in Berlin in den 90er Jahren entwerfen zu können, bedarf es einer Vorstellung von der Zukunft der europäischen Stadt und ihrer Architektur.

Landscape has become synonymous with systems which follow no obvious hierarchy, where the individual element is a constituent part and generator of the whole. Landscape implies excessive formal complexity, fore- and background in flux.

Im England des 18. Jahrhunderts nahm der Begriff der "Landschaft" eine weitere Bedeutung an: Die "Country"-Partei, die in Opposition zur autoritären Herrschaft Georg des I. gegründet wurde, bediente sich der buchstäblichen Analogie zwischen ihren liberalen politischen Zielen und der Natur der englischen Landschaft.

.

Hence – in reverse – the constructed nature of the English landscape garden became the manifestation (the medium) of a particular political and philosophical programme.

Landscape in dreams represents (according to C.G.Jung) the unknown; in our conscious symbology it is more often associated with individual freedom (which is continuously exploited by advertising imagery today).

In England of the 18th century "landscape" invited a political analogy: the "Country" Party – founded in opposition to the authoritarian rule of George I. – saw a direct parallel between its liberal political aims and the nature of the English countryside.

Umgekehrt wurde die künstliche Natur des englischen Landschaftsgartens zur Manifestation und zum Medium eines politischen und philosophischen Programms.

Landscape is associated with things alive. Landscape seems to suggest growth and decay, the cycle of the day and the season, in short ...continuous change.

Der Ort, an dem Architektur zumeist gebaut wird, hat sich jenseits ihrer traditionellen Parameter verändert, ohne ihre funktionale und räumliche Definition scheint sich "Stadt" in "das Stadthafte" verändert zu haben, eine weitgehend nicht sichtbare Lebensform, ein menschlicher Agglomeratszustand. Umgekehrt hat sich "das Land" – traditionellerweise das Gegenteil der Stadt (zumindest in Westeuropa) – in eine Variation desselben Zustandes verwandelt.

We distrust the concept of continuity, particularly in the context of Berlin, and would welcome intelligent newness.

The area beyond the traditional parameters within which most architecture is being built is changing. Having lost its functional and spatial definition, "city" seems to have become "cityness", an almost invisible mode of existence, a human agglomerate condition. Similarly the countryside – the city's traditional antagonist – has become (certainly as far as Western Europe is concerned) merely a mild variation of the same non-entity.

Wir mißtrauen dem Konzept von der Kontinuität, insbesondere in Berlin, und würden intelligentes Neues vorziehen.

Die Interpretation der zeitgenössischen Stadt als Landschaft (innerhalb und außerhalb der Verwaltungseinheit) erlaubt uns, die sich verändernde Ordnung der gebauten Umgebung in einem neuen Licht zu sehen: was zunächst nur als Schwäche gesehen wurde, kann nun als positive Qualität verstanden werden.

Seeing the contemporary city as a landscape (both within and without the limits of the administrative unit of a town) helps to see the changing order of the built environment in a new light: one begins to appreciate as a quality what has up to then been perceived only as a weakness.

Urbanität kann – unserer Meinung nach – nur ein Maß kultureller Verfeinerung in der städtischen Sphäre sein, Urbanität braucht keine Ideologie.

Architektur galt simultan als Manifestation und Artikulation des sozialen und kulturellen Hintergrunds, in dem sie entsteht. In der heutigen, sich schnell ändernden Gesellschaft ist Architektur als Ausdrucksmittel marginalisiert und zum größten Teil durch schnell reagierende, weit verbreitete und extrem beeinflussende Medien wie Fernsehen, Film und Druck ersetzt worden.

Urbanity – in our view – can only be a measure of cultural refinement of the urban environment, urbanity is free of ideology.

Bedeutungsträger ist in der heutigen Kultur in erster Linie das Bild. Oberflächlich gesehen ist die Landschaft der Stadt eine Landschaft der Bilder.

In der Wahrnehmung unserer Umwelt heute ist die Erfahrung des Films nicht wegzudenken. Um zur physischen Welt zurückzufinden, wäre der bewußte Rückzug aus der fiktiven Welt der Medien notwendig.

Architecture used to manifest the social and cultural background into which it is embedded (and which it articulates at the same time). However, in today's diverse and fast changing society, architecture has widely been marginalised and replaced by ephemeral, fast reacting, wide-spread and extremely powerful media such as TV, film, and newspapers. The medium of today's culture is first of all the image. Superficially the landscape of the city has become one of images.

Der Landschaftsgarten des 18. Jahrhunderts war – einem primitiven Film vergleichbar – als gebaute Sequenz von Bildern konzipiert, die in der bewegten Wahrnehmung zu einer zusammenhängenden Geschichte verschmelzen sollten.

The spatial order of the 18th century landscape garden was conceived as a built sequence of paintings which – in movement – should fuse into a story as in a primitive film.

The perception of today's "real" environment has become indivisable from the experience of film. To rediscover the physical world the deliberate withdrawal from the ficticious world of the media seems necessary.

Trotz allem bildet Architektur – mehr denn je –
die Umwelt, in der unser Leben stattfindet.
Sie bildet das Territorium und die Hülle allen
sozialen Austausches. Die Flüchtigkeit ihrer
Bildhaftigkeit steht im starken Kontrast zur
physischen Präsenz ihres Körpers.

*However – more than ever – architecture is
the environment in which our life takes place.
It still provides the territory and the envelope
to all social activity. The immateriality of its
image stands in contrast to the physicality of
its body.*

Gleichermaßen "wirklich" und "fiktiv", abstrakt
und konkret ist die Stadt wie ein Medium auf
der Suche nach seiner Bedeutung.

*Certainly able to shape our life on every level,
architecture's beauty is to make visibility
work and physicality speak.*

*Simultaneously "real" and "ficticious", abstract
and concrete, the city has become a medium in
search (but without need) of a message.*

Mit Sicherheit ist Architektur in der Lage,
unser Leben in jeder Hinsicht zu gestalten.
Ihre Schönheit bringt Sichtbarkeit zum Funktionieren und Körperlichkeit zum Sprechen.

gsw hauptverwaltung · gsw headquarters · 1991

aufgabe
Neubau und Erweiterung der Hauptverwaltung
der Gemeinnützigen Siedlungs- und Wohnungs-
baugesellschaft mbH, Berlin
umfang
ca. 30.000 m^2 Büros, Läden
und öffentliche Flächen
standort
Kochstraße, Berlin-Kreuzberg

brief
*Extension to the headquarters building of the
Gemeinnützige Siedlungs- und Wohnungsbau-
gesellschaft mbH, Berlin*
size
*approx. 30,000 m^2 office,
commercial and public space*
site
Kochstrasse, Berlin-Kreuzberg

Dieses Projekt erweitert ein Bürohochhaus
aus den Fünfzigern: Das "Graphische und
Gewerbezentrum (GGZ)" war eines der ersten
Wiederaufbauprojekte in der (ursprünglich
barocken) Friedrichstadt. In seiner bewußten
Ablehnung der Stadt des 18. und 19. Jahrhunderts sollte das Punkthochhaus einen äußeren
und inneren Neuanfang demonstrieren: Es ver-
körperte die Hoffnung auf eine moderne Kapi-
tale, die aus der Asche der zerstörten Reichs-
hauptstadt auferstehen sollte.

Durch den Bau der Mauer blieb diese "optimi-
stische Initiative" unvollendet. Die "demokrati-
sche Stadt" bleibt nur ein Bruchstück in einem
Feld, das von den Spuren unterschiedlicher
Stadtideen gezeichnet ist.

Der Entwurf bemüht sich, diese Fragmente zu
einem dreidimensionalen Gebilde zusammen-
zuflechten und damit nicht nur den Neubauteil
sondern auch den "Affront" der fünfziger Jahre
in das Gefüge der Stadt zu integrieren, ohne
die Absichten der Wiederaufbaugeneration zu
untergraben.

*This project is an extension of a 1950's office
tower: the existing "Graphische und Gewerbezentrum" was one of the first post-war reconstruction projects in (the originally baroque)
Friedrichstadt. In its deliberate opposition
to the city of the 18th and 19th centuries it
clearly intended to demonstrate a new beginning. It manifested the hope for a modern
metropolis to rise out of the ashes of the de-
stroyed capital of the Reich.*

*However, the construction of the Wall inter-
cepted this "optimistic initative". Instead of
the democratic city the area around the
border remained a field filled with different
city-fragments.*

*The scheme ties these fragments into a
three-dimensional whole, and tries not only to
introduce the new buildings but also to retroactively integrate the "affront" of the 1950's
without undermining its original intentions.*

ggz grundsteinlegung 1957
ggz laying the foundation stone 1957

isometrie der südlichen friedrichstadt
isometric of southern friedrichstadt

gsw hauptverwaltung
gsw headquarters · 1991

Der Erweiterungsbau geht eine Verbindung mit dem Bestand ein, der das Konglomerat unterschiedlicher Elemente als Wachstumsmodell einer Stadt nicht nur akzeptiert, sondern zum Ordnungsprinzip erhöht. Das neue Ensemble reagiert auf die barocke Logik des Stadtgrundrißes ebenso wie auf die Regeln der Verdichtung im 19. Jahrhundert. Es absorbiert die Objekthaftigkeit des bestehenden Gebäudes und registriert das Motiv des "Dialoges über die Mauer" – der Konfrontation von Hochhäusern über den Raum der Mauer hinweg, der ein direktes Resultat des kalten Krieges war.

In dieser beinahe didaktischen Kombination verschiedener Typen verschiedener Generationen ist natürlich die neue Hochhausscheibe der Gebäudeteil, den wir am meisten mit der Gegenwart (und der Zukunft) assoziieren. Unsere Bemühungen galten hier einerseits der Aufgabe "Arbeitsplatz in der Stadt" und andererseits einer Architektur, die im Eingehen auf die (gebaute und natürliche) Umwelt sparsam mit Energien umgeht.

The extension forming a whole with the existing does not just accept the conglomerate of heterogenous parts as a model for growth, but formalizes it as a principle for the order of this particular part of Berlin. The new ensemble reacts to the baroque plan as much as to the 19th century construction rules; it absorbs the object quality of the 1950's building and registers what we called the "dialogue across the Wall" – the confrontation of high-rise buildings across the wall which is an urban figure directly resulting from the period of the cold war.

In this almost didactic combination of building elements from different periods it is obviously the new (high-rise) slab which we associate most with the present and the future. Here we set ourselves the brief to create exemplary workplaces in the city on the one hand, and on the other we were looking for an architecture which, as it coalesces with the built and natural environment, expends energy sparingly.

perspektivskizze
sketch perspective

wettbewerbsmodell 1991
competition model 1991

24

panorama vom bestehenden gebäude aus
panorama from existing building

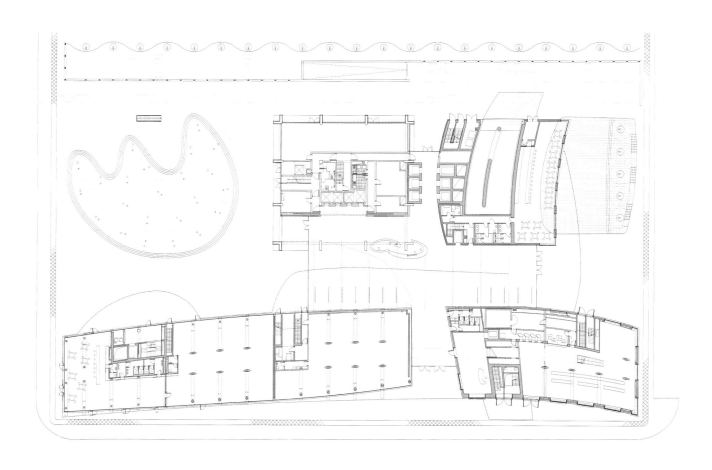

grundriß erdgeschoß
ground floor plan

studie eingangshalle
entrance hall study

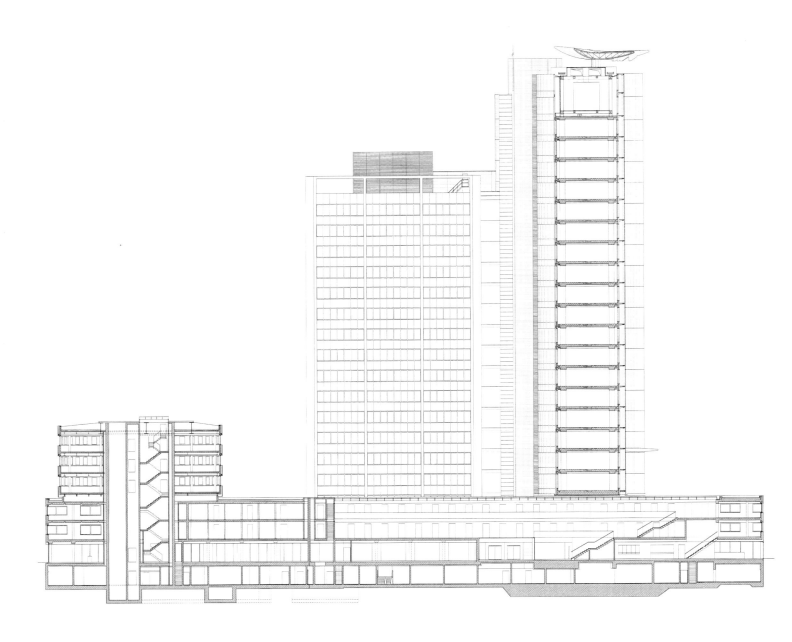

schnitt durch atrium
section through atrium

studie atrium
atrium study

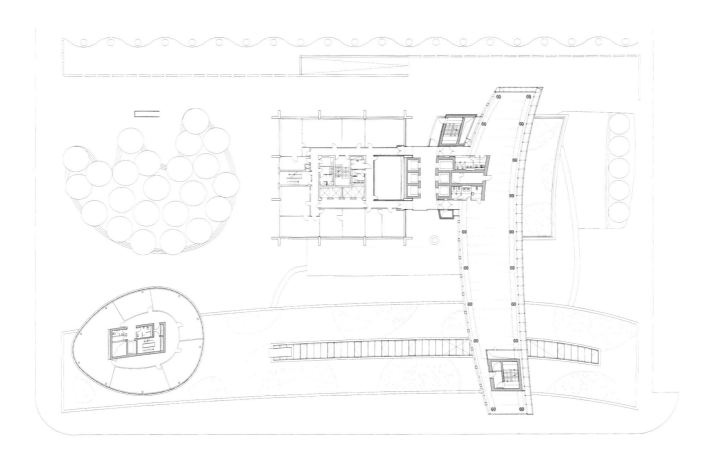

grundriß normalgeschoß
typical floor plan

32

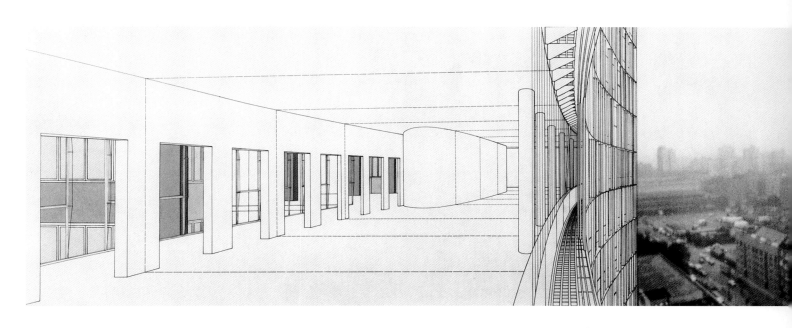

innenperspektive büro
office interior

modellansicht west
model from west

modellausschnitt fassade
façade detail

olympische schwimm- und radsporthallen
olympic swimming and cycling halls · 1992

olympische schwimm-
und radsporthallen
olympic swimming and
cycling halls · 1992

aufgabe
Olympische Sporthallen für die olympischen
Wettbewerbe im Schwimmen und Radsport
umfang
ca. 85.000 m²
standort
Am Ringbahngraben zwischen den Bezirken
Prenzlauer Berg und Friedrichshain

brief
*Sports halls for the olympic
swimming and cycling competitions*
size
approx. 85.000 m²
site
*At the S-Bahn moat between the boroughs
of Prenzlauer Berg and Friedrichshain*

In einem Feld zwischen gegensätzlichen städtischen Texturen (Block und Straße auf der
einen und "Objekte im fließenden Raum" auf
der anderen Seite) wird das große Gebäude der
Sporthallen als ein "Klimaterritorium" definiert,
das sich in eine Kette von Stadtparks zwischen
dem existierenden Volkspark Friedrichshain
und dem Prenzlauer Berg eingliedert.

Die Einbindung eines so großen Gebäudes
in die städtische Landschaft wird durch die
"ordnende" Einführung eines kreuzförmigen
Gebäudes erreicht, das bislang unartikulierte
Stadtbereiche in klar definierte Territorien
unterteilt: jeder Quadrant enthält eine andere
Rolle, Funktion und Identität (Olympiapark,
Dienstleistungszentrum/Stadtplatz und Woh-
nungsquartier) die sich (auch zeitlich) unabhängig voneinander entwickeln können.

*Placed between opposing city fragments –
one generated by "espace poché" (19th
century) the other made of objects within
unlimited space (20th century) – the scheme
unfolds a logic of territories to create a
"playing-field" which ties Volkspark
Friedrichshain and the park at Prenzlauer
Berg into a chain of park-events. In this
context the large building of the sports halls
is conceived of as a "climate territory".*

*The integration of the very large building
into the urban landscape is achieved through
the ordering device of a building cross, which
subdivides hitherto unarticulated areas into
clearly defined territories. Each quadrant
fulfills a different rôle, function and identity
(Olympic park, service centre, city square,
residential quarter). This allows the quadrants
to develop independently from one another.*

stadt fragmente
city fragments

lageplan
site plan

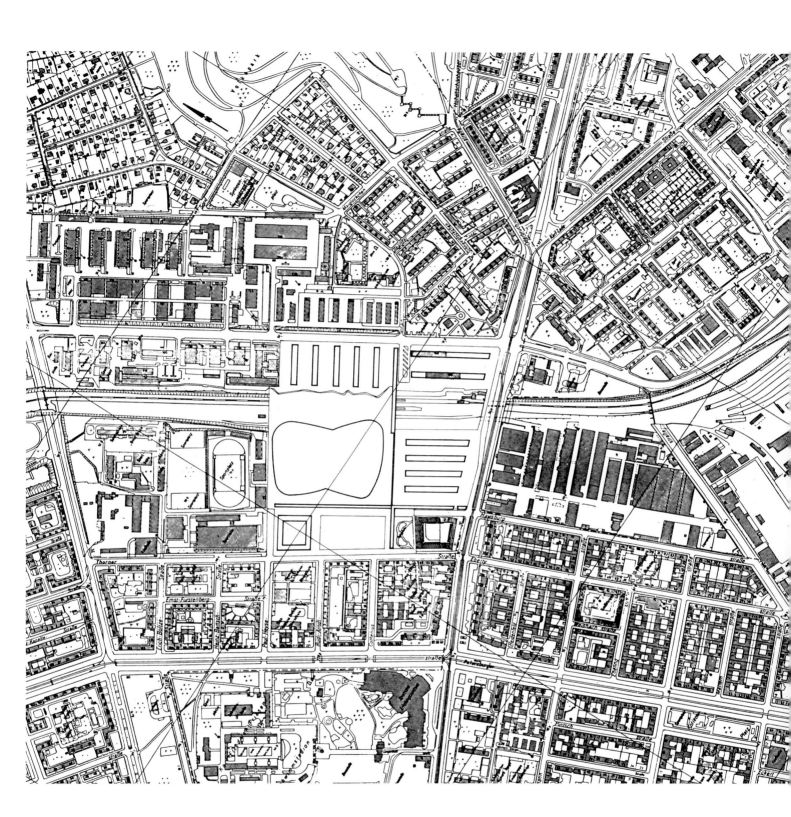

olympische schwimm-
und radsporthallen
olympic swimming and
cycling halls · 1992

Das Gebäude selbst besteht aus einem "modellierten Gelände" unter einem Dach, das als "technische Wolke" den Ort überdeckt und sein Klima konditioniert. In dem bis zu fünf Meter hohen Tragwerk ist die Technik untergebracht, die Heizung, Lüftung, Wärmerückgewinnung, Entfeuchtung, Beschallung etc. übernimmt.

Ihre Stromversorgung erhält die "Wolke" aus einem Sonnenkraftwerk, das in seine ca. drei Hektar große Außenhaut integriert ist.

The sports building itself consists of a continuous ground surface – moulded into shape to create pools and racing track – which is protected by a "technical cloud". This cloud is constructed of steel and glass, approximately three hectares in size, which conditions the interior climate of the building; it contains space heating, ventilation machinery, heat recuperation and dehumidification plant, sound systems etc.

All services are run through a photovoltaic power plant integrated into its top surface.

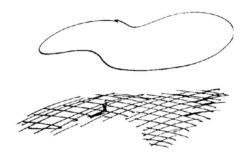

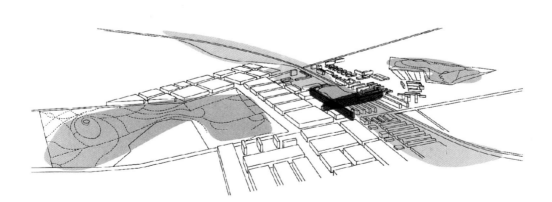

wolkenskizze
cloud sketch

geländeperspektive
aerial view

konzeptmodell
concept model

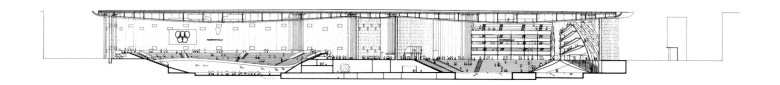

schnitt
section

grundriß
plan

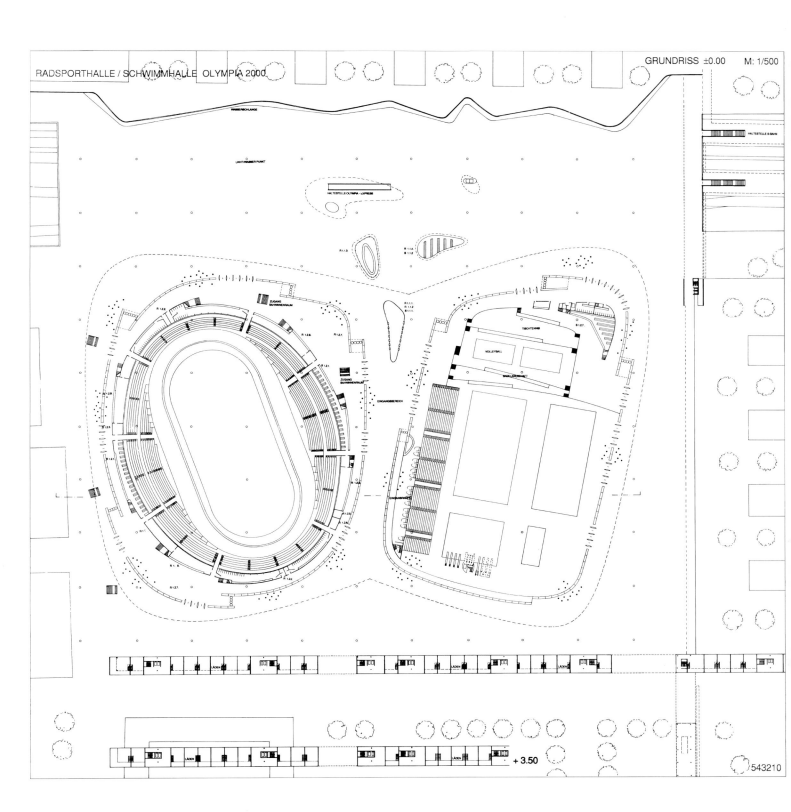

RADSPORTHALLE / SCHWIMMHALLE OLYMPIA 2000

GRUNDRISS ±0.00   M: 1/500

+ 3.50

543210

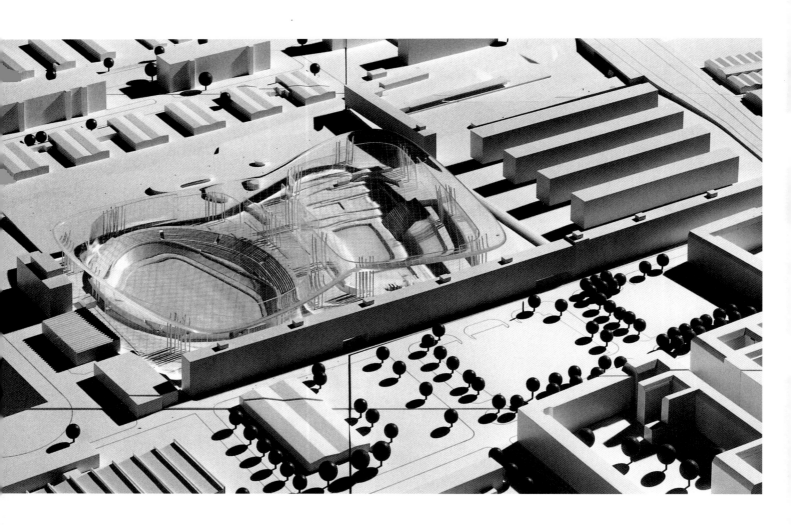

modell
model

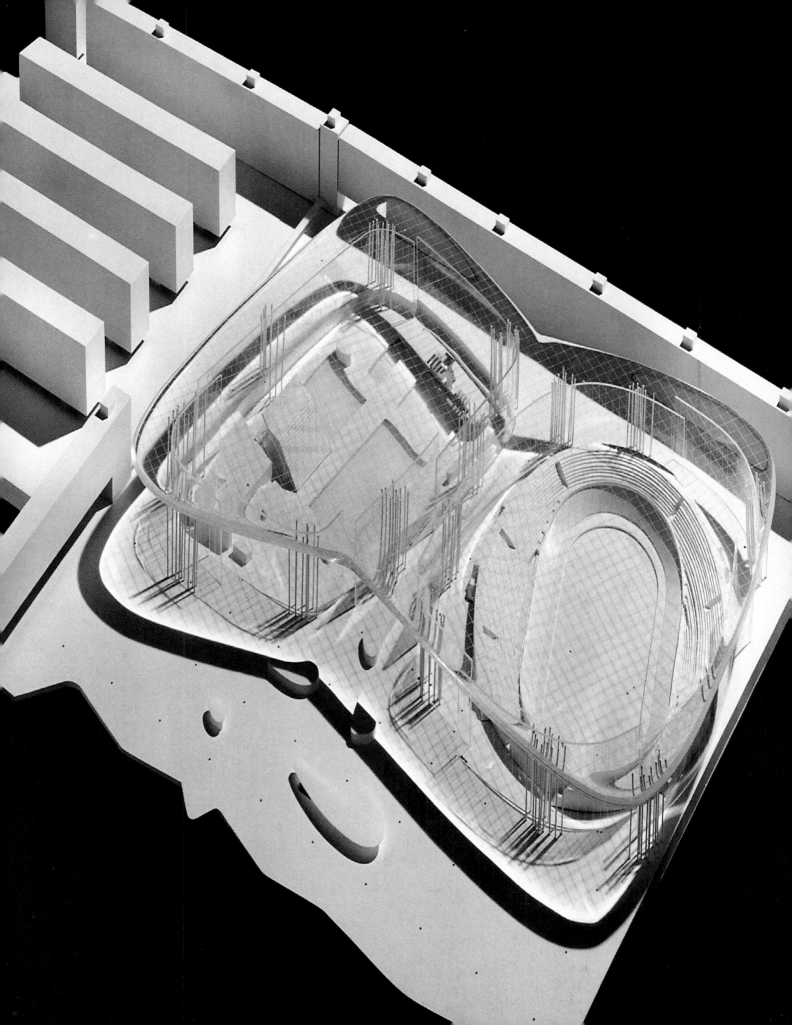

heinrich heine strasse · 1993

heinrich heine strasse
1993

aufgabe
Städtebaulicher Rahmenplan für die
Bebauung des ehemaligen Mauerstreifens
umfang
ca. 15 ha
standort
Ehemaliger Grenzübergang
Heinrich Heine Straße
(Checkpoint Delta)

brief
Masterplan for the development of
the landstrip left by the Berlin Wall
size
approx. 15 acr.
site
The former checkpoint
"Heinrich Heine Strasse"
(Checkpoint Delta)

Das Projektgebiet liegt an einer Stelle, an der vier verschiedene städtebauliche Leitmotive nebeneinander existieren: Der barocke Stadt-plan im Norden trifft auf eine Gartenstadt aus den fünfziger Jahren dieses Jahrhunderts. Die Heinrich Heine Straße selbst – als großzü-giger Stadt-Boulevard nie ganz vollendet – wird auf der Ostseite von einem riesigen Neu-bauquartier flankiert, das nach den Prinzipien der "cité contemporaine" angelegt zu sein scheint; dies steht wiederum dem steinernen Berlin mit Block und Straße gegenüber. Da-zwischen klafft eine große Lücke, wo einst die Grenzanlagen standen.

Der Entwurf schlägt zunächst vor, jedes der Stadtelemente für sich zu verstärken: Der Boulevard wird vervollständigt und von zweigeschossigen "beams" flankiert, die hel-fen, die breite Straße zur Flaniermeile zu machen. In der "cité contemporaine" werden Innenhöfe völlig von Autos befreit und statt-dessen großzügige Gärten angelegt. Für die Quartiere des 19. Jahrhunderts gilt Lücken-schließung und Reparatur, für die Gartenstadt in erster Linie Renovation der öffentlichen Grünräume.

The site is located at the junction of four different urban leitmotivs. The baroque city plan in the north (tracing the original fortifi-cation border of Cölln/Berlin) was divided from the 19th century "stony Berlin" of block-and-street firstly by WW II bombs and sub-sequently by the Berlin Wall. The western and eastern parts of the city then each developed their versions of the garden city in the 1950's and 1960's respectively. In addition, that part of Heinrich Heine Strasse lying to the east (the majority) was projected as a grand boule-vard (but never completed), and is itself flanked by a quarter seemingly designed along the principles of Corb's "cité contempo-raine". The recent removal of the Wall and the ensuing exposure and giving-back-to-the-city of the land left fallow between the sides further underlines the extraordinary multi-plicity of city-typologies in such a small area.

Firstly the design proposes to reinforce each urban element in its own right. Heinrich Heine Boulevard is to be completed and flanked on either side by two-storey beam-buildings which help to narrow the giant section into a space more likely to attract the flaneur. In the "cité contemporaine" the exterior spaces are to be cleared of parked cars in order to develop generous landscaping. The 19th century quarters are being repaired and

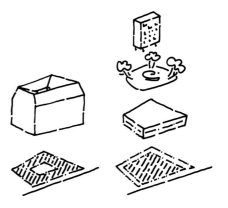

mauerviertel
metropolitan village

stadtarchipel
city archipelago

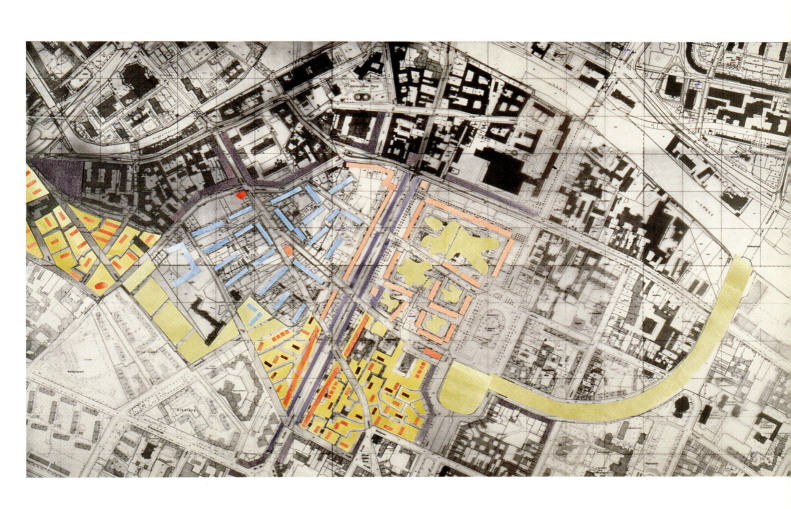

Das Konglomerat dieser Stadtteile, die jeweils Spiegelbilder der Lebensvorstellung bestimmter historischer Abschnitte sind, soll dann durch eine Bebauung im ehemaligen Mauerstreifen ergänzt werden, die als Ausdruck des sozialen und kulturellen Kontextes der neunziger Jahre erkennbar sein soll.

Aus Vorgefundenem konstituiert, bildet die vorgeschlagene Figur eine deutlich neue Struktur: Der Grundriß baut auf der existierenden Topographie von Straße und Parzelle auf, wobei das historische Bebauungsmuster umgekehrt wurde: anstatt die Gebäude mit einer Brandwand an die Grundstücksgrenze heranzubauen, wird hier vorgeschlagen, die Mitte der Parzelle mit einem zweigeschoßigen Sockelbau zu belegen, der rundherum einen der Bauordnung entsprechenden Abstand zur Grundstücksgrenze einhält. Dadurch entstehen im Muster der historischen Parzellen "mews"-ähnliche Zwischenräume, die ein internes Erschließungsnetz bilden.

completed, and the garden city is to be carefully condensed and renewed. The conglomerate of these fragments – each a mirror image of the lifestyles and aspirations of its period – is proposed to be complemented (in the vacuum left by the Wall) by a part which expresses the social and cultural conditions of the 1990's.

The proposal reinterprets the existing in its reconstitution of "found" elements, but at the same time the plan adds a recognisably new figure to its context. The conventional topography of the street with its historic landparcels is inverted. Instead of placing a fire wall around the site-line (from which the building would develop towards the centre of the site, leaving as small a lightwell or courtyard as possible), a double-storey plinth-building is placed in the centre of the plot (maintaining the legally required distance from the site border) thus creating – by default – mews-like spaces which follow the pattern of the historic land divisions, and which become the means of access to the new area.

photos wettbewerbsgebiet
site photogaphs

doppelseite: isometrische zeichnung
overleaf: isometric painting

Versucht der Grundriß eine Reinterpretation der historischen Stadttopographie, so schlägt der Schnitt eine Reinterpretation der "Kreuzberger Mischung" von Wohnen und Arbeiten in einem Gebäude vor. Was im historischen Typ jedoch in einem Volumen untergebracht war (und dementsprechend für territoriale Konflikte sorgte), ist hier durch die klare Artikulation in Schichten entzerrt.
Während die unteren Etagen ausschließlich dem Gewerbe vorbehalten sind, werden die Dächer der zweigeschoßigen Sockelbauten als durchgehende Grünflächen angelegt, die zum Grundstück für eine zweite, sechsgeschoßige (Wohn-) Bebauung werden.

Bei funktionaler Trennung erlaubt das Modell die unmittelbare Gleichzeitigkeit von Wohnen und Arbeiten, "Stadt" und "Land", "Innen-" und "Vorstadt" in einer urbanen Komposition.

While the plan proposes a reinterpretation of the pattern of land use, the section proposes a reinterpretation of the "Kreuzberg" mixture, a coexistence of living and work. However, what was at one time accommodated in a single volume (creating the well documented conflicts) has been clearly separated in section: the roofs of the double-storey commercial buildings are designed to be continuous gardens which become the site for a second layer of residential buildings. Flats are accommodated in generously spaced six-storey slabs, amongst which are found the usual services associated with residential development (such as kindergartens etc.).

Despite the functional separation the model allows for the simultaneity of housing and work, of city and country, suburb and inner city, closeness and distance in one urban composition.

typischer grundriß
typical plan

56

metropolitan village

59

stadtmitte marzahn · city centre marzahn · 1994

stadtmitte marzahn
city centre marzahn
1994

aufgabe
Städtebaulicher Rahmenplan für die
Entwicklung der Mitte der Großsiedlung;
Entwurf eines Kaufhauses
umfang
36 ha
standort
Marzahner Promenade

brief
*Masterplan for the development of a
city centre for the new-town of Marzahn;
design for a department store*
size
36 acr.
site
Marzahner Promenade

Marzahn ist die größte Neubausiedlung der
ehemaligen DDR. Für die einst als renommier-
ten Stadtteil bevorzugte Wohnadresse bedeutete die Wiedervereinigung eine schwere Iden-
titätskrise.
Die Bewohner, die nicht sofort in den Westen
aufbrachen, kämpfen heute gegen eine stei-
gende Ghettoisierung. Was einst in seiner Tota-
lität "Eigentum des Volkes" war, wird jetzt nach
den Prinzipien kapitalistischer Grundstücks-
wirtschaft zerlegt. Die vorhandene soziale
Infrastruktur (Kindergärten, Jugendclubs,
Schulen, Nachbarschafts-Cafés, etc.) wurde
vielfach zerstört und wird nun sukzessive
durch kommerzielle Unternehmen ersetzt.
Privatisierung, Individualisierung und die damit
verbundene Arbeitslosigkeit und andere
soziale Probleme halten Einzug in einen nach
Vorstellungen einer kollektiven Existenz
geplanten und unterhaltenen Stadtteil.

Die Aufgabe, in dieser Situation ein neues
Stadtzentrum zu definieren, verlangt einerseits
nach der physischen und symbolischen Manifestation einer "Neuen Ära". Andererseits wäre
der Ansatz, den Charakter von Marzahn mit
einer Einzelmaßnahme grundsätzlich zu verän-
dern, ebenso vermessen wie aussichtslos.

Anstatt die zweifelsfrei mangelhafte Situation
mit ihr fremden Bildern zu überschwemmen,
wurde deshalb eine Strategie vorgeschlagen,
wie sich innerhalb der Spielregeln des Ist-Zu-
standes neues Leben entfalten kann. Die Lösung der Einzelaufgaben wurde als der Beginn
eines Prozesses gesehen, aus dem sich die
Identität des Ortes allmählich heranbilden wird.

*Marzahn is the largest new town of the for-
mer DDR. Highly acclaimed during the socialist period, today the area is suffering from a
deep identity crisis. Those inhabitants who
have not yet left for the West are today fight-
ing an increasing ghettoisation.
What used to be "the property of the people" in
its entirety is now being disected according to
the principles of capitalist market economy.
Existing social infrastructure (kindergartens,
youth clubs, schools, community centres, etc.)
have been closed down, and are successively
being replaced by commercial enterprise.
Privatisation, individualisation and conse-
quently unemployment and other social problems are infiltrating an environment which
was designed with a collective existence in
mind.*

*The brief to articulate a new city centre for
this situation seemed to request a physical
manifestation of the "new era" on the one
hand. On the other hand the attempt to com-
pletely change the character of Marzahn with
a few single interventions seemed as arrogant
as it seemed hopeless.*

*Instead of flooding the (indisputably faulty)
existing situation with irrelevant images,
the scheme proposes a strategy for a new life
to develop within the rules of the existing. The
resolution of individual problems is the
beginning of a process-as-catalyst which will
slowly build a new identity.*

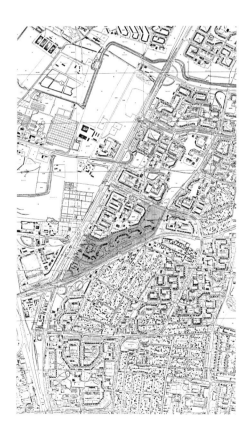

stadt marzahn (170.000 einwohner)
the city of marzahn (170,000 inhabitants)

luftaufnahme des wettbewerbsgeländes
aerial photograph of competition site

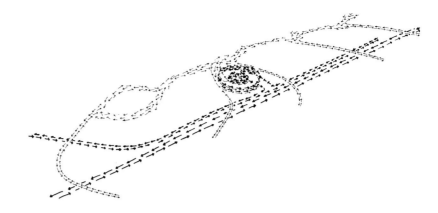

Der Entwurf schlägt vor:

• Nord- und Süd-Marzahn mehrfach über die vierspurige Landsberger Allee hinweg miteinander zu verbinden. (Diese Fußgänger-/Radfahrerbrücken bieten dann erste Kristallisationspunkte, an denen weitere Funktionen angesiedelt werden).

• Die bestehende Trennung der Promenade in zwei Zonen zu verstärken. Während die tiefer gelegte Ebene als Zugang für die Wohnhäuser am nördlichen Ende dient, funktioniert der höher gelegene Bereich als Einkaufs-Straße. Durch die Einfügung einer dreigeschoßigen "Schlange" mit Büros und Läden, soll eine Verdichtung erreicht werden, die die existierende räumliche Situation durch dynamische Elemente artikuliert und aufwertet.

• An beiden Enden der Einkaufspromenade die existierenden Platzsituationen zu vervollständigen.

• Die bestehende Verkehrsführung und offene Parkplatzanlagen zu rationalisieren und Parkflächen, Einkaufspromenade sowie Erschliessungsstraße mit gärtnerischen und baulichen Mitteln in eine vielfältige Landschaft zu verwandeln und das Kaufhaus "Karstadt" als Bestandteil dieser Landschaft zu konzipieren.

The proposals are:

• To connect the northern and southern parts of Marzahn with footbridges across the four-laned Landsberger Allee. These will establish points of focus which will attract further activities.

• To reinforce the existing separation of the "Promenade" into two zones. The lower half serves as access to the housing on the northern edge, whilst the upper half at the moment is a one-sided shopping street. Through the introduction of a three-storey "snake" building (whose upper two stories are to be built and let as fragments, and whose lower storey is to be left open to accomodate non-institutionalised activities), the existing shopping street is completed and condensed, and the spatial situation is enriched through the introduction of an interstitial and dynamic element.

• To complete the head and tail of the "snake" into clearly articulated spaces.

• To rationalise the existing traffic pattern and to convert (through building and planting) open areas and parking lots, shopping street and access road into a rich landscape of many uses and clearly defined territories, and to design the Karstadt department store as part of this landscape.

fahr- und fußgängerverkehr
pedestrian and vehicular circulation

Der Entwurf des Kaufhauses verdeutlicht die dem Gesamtkonzept zugrundeliegende Mentalität. Anstelle der sonst üblichen "Box" mit Parkplätzen auf dem Dach (oder im Keller), der ein "modernes"/technisches/historisches Kleid angezogen wird, besteht das Kaufhaus hier aus zwei miteinander verschränkten Spiralrampen, auf denen simultan geparkt und eingekauft wird.

Das Kaufhaus wird damit zum Treffpunkt zweier am Ort vorhandener Bewegungsarten und Stadtelemente. Architektur wird als ein Mittel des "Behausens" und "Ermöglichens", nicht als Monument verstanden. Die Unverwechselbarkeit und Präsenz des Ortes entspringt der unerwarteten Reinterpretation des Bestehenden bei gleichzeitiger, simpler Erfüllung der anstehenden Aufgaben.

The design of this department store illustrates the attitude at the base of the whole concept: instead of the otherwise usual shopping-cum-parking "box" clad in a modern/ technical/historical dress, here the department store is conceived as a set of interlocking spiral ramps which simultaneously accomodate both shopping and parking activities.

The department store thus becomes the meeting point of two existing rituals of use and of two urban elements. Architecture is understood to be a means of "housing" and "enabling", and not as a monument. The identity and presence of the place is a result of an unexpected reinterpretation of the existing, and the straightforward resolution of problems and tasks at hand.

perspektive kaufhaus
department store perspective

doppelseite: isometrische zeichnung
overleaf: isometric painting

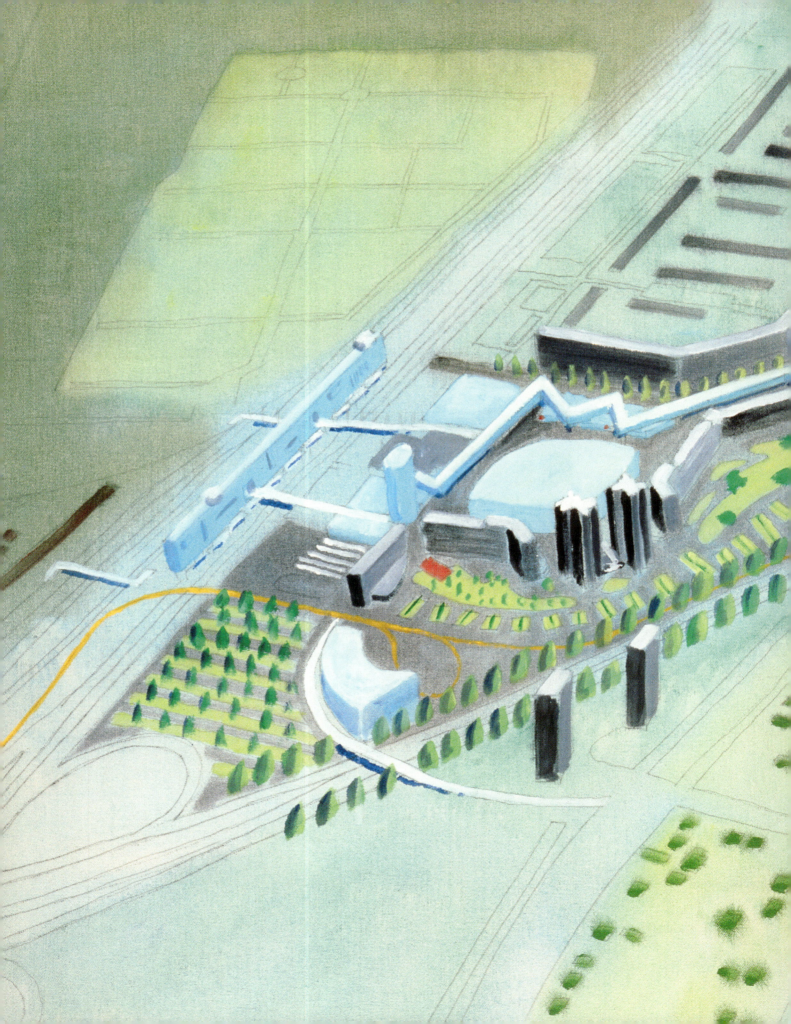

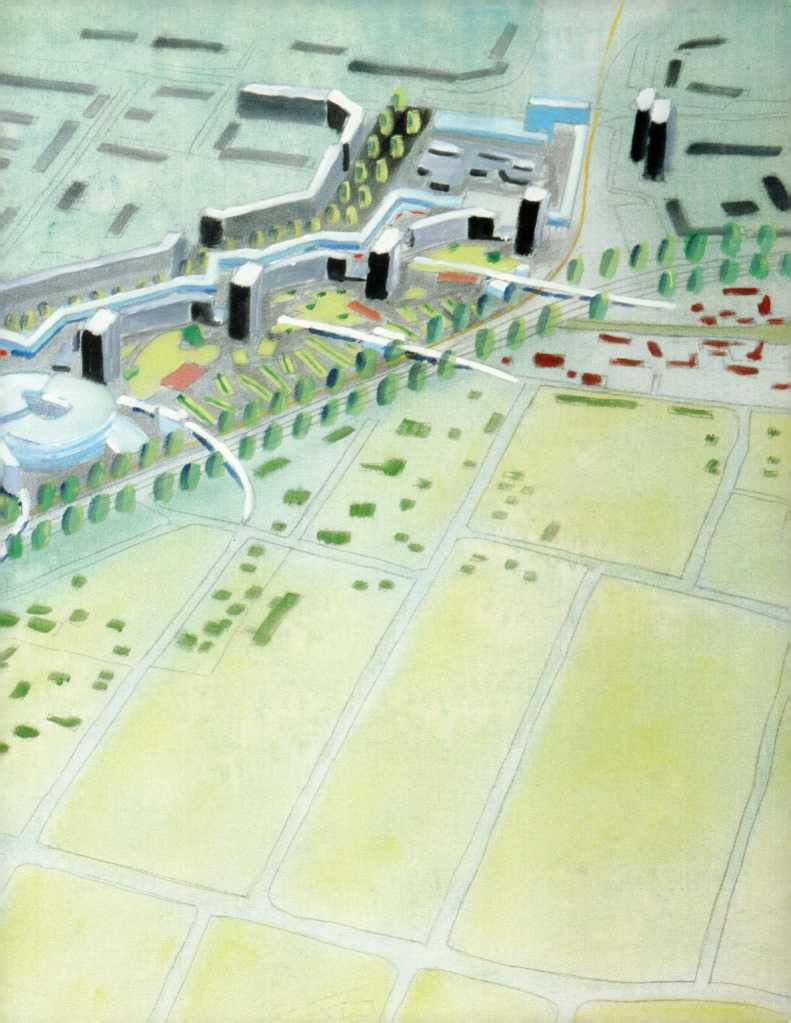

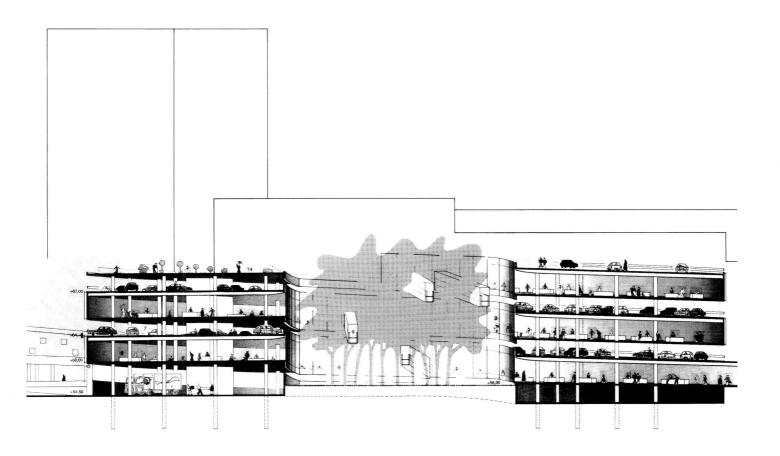

kaufhaus modell
department store model

kaufhaus schnitt
department store section

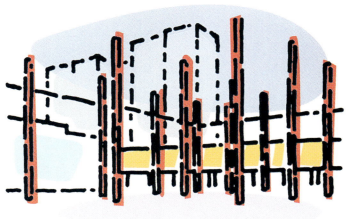

blicksequenz entlang der neuen promenade
sequence of views along the renewed promenade

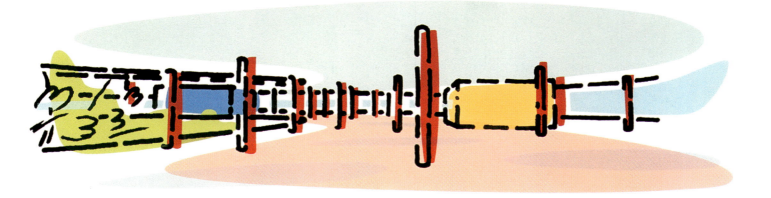

innenraum kaufhaus
department store interior

wohnhaus und bürohaus in marzahn · apartment house and office building · 1994

wohnhaus und bürohaus in marzahn
apartment house and office building
1994

aufgabe
Hauptverwaltung der Wohnungsbau-
gesellschaft Marzahn sowie Entwurf
eines Wohngebäudes
umfang
ca. 5.500 m² Bürofläche, 130 Wohnungen
standort
Großsiedlung Marzahn

brief
*Office Headquarters for the Marzahn
Housing Association and proposal for a
residential building*
size
approx. 5.500 m² office area, 130 flats
site
The new town of Marzahn

Die Gebäudetypologien der Großsiedlung
Marzahn sind in der Regel freistehende Riegel
oder Türme, die so angeordnet sind, daß sie
Raumfiguren wie zum Beispiel "Gevierte" bilden. Diese Inseln des (Halb-) Privaten schwimmen in einem Meer räumlich nicht näher defi-
nierter Zonen, die in erster Linie dem ruhenden
und fahrenden Verkehr dienen.

Der Entwurf unternimmt die Reinterpretation
dieser vorhandenen Landschaft von "Objekten
und Territorien", um mit neuen Räumen die
bestehende Struktur abzurunden: Zur Ergän-
zung einer Ecksituation an einer der Haupt-
straßen im Gebiet, werden zwei Gebäudepaare
aus jeweils einem (Gebäude-) Körper und
einer (gebauten) Fläche vorgeschlagen. Die
Körper formen Blickpunkte und Raumkanten,
die Flächen Territorien und territoriale
Begrenzungen.
Eines der beiden neuen Häuser enthält Wohnungen; die dazugehörige "Fläche" ist ein Ga-
ragengebäude mit einer Dachterrasse, die als
"Garten der vier Jahreszeiten" konzipiert ist.

*Buildings in the new town of Marzahn are
almost always free-standing slabs or towers,
which are arranged to form spatial enclosures
(such as squares etc.). The resulting territories of (semi-) privacy are floating in a sea of
undetermined space – which is mostly dedi-
cated to moving traffic and parked vehicles.*

*The design, in attempting a regeneration of
this existing typology of "object and territory",
follows an approach similar to that of "Stadtmitte Marzahn", in that the proposal aims to
follow the "genius loci" of the place (instead of
superimposing an alien ordering system).
For an existing corner situation at a junction
of a main road and a linear park, are proposed two building pairs, each consisting of
a tall house and a "blanket".
The tall buildings form view points and
spaces, whilst the "blankets" create territories and territorial definitions (fences).*

photo des wettbewerbsgeländes
competition site photograph

territorien
territories

wohnhaus und bürohaus in marzahn
apartment house and office building
1994

Das zweite Haus ist ein Bürogebäude. Das hierzu gehörige Flachgebäude enthält Läden und weitere Parkplätze; auf seinem Dach befinden sich eine Tennisanlage und ein Café. Beide "Körper" sind in ihrem Volumen mit den vorgefundenen Hochhäusern identisch. Im Gegensatz zu den Nachbarn bietet das Wohngebäude jedoch klar orientierte Grundrisse, die in Nord-Süd Richtung zoniert sind.

Als äußerste Zone der Wohnungen bildet auch die Südfassade einen Raum: Zwischen einer einfachen, zu öffnenden Glashaut (als Wetterschutz) und einer zweiten, leichten (und wärmegedämmten) Wand entsteht ein saisonal unterschiedlich nutzbarer Bereich für Wintergärten, Küchen, Spielzimmer etc.. Materialität und Farbe dieser Zone (und damit der Südfassade) sind der Gestaltung der einzelnen Mieter überlassen.

Das Bürohochhaus ist als ein Gebäude mit intelligenter Klimahülle entworfen: Ein massiver Kern wird durchgehend von einer Doppelfassade umschlossen, die Aufwärmung, Abkühlung, Be- und Entlüftung des Gebäudes kontrolliert und Möglichkeiten gibt, das Tageslicht optimal zu nutzen. Die Primärkonstruktion selbst fungiert als Zuluftkanal sowie als Wärme- bzw. als Kühlespeicher.

One of the two tall houses contains flats; its blanket is designed as a "garden of the four seasons" under which a garage building is sheltered. The other tall building is an office tower; its low-rise structure contains shops and further parking facilities, with tennis courts and a café on the roof. Together the "blankets" define a triangular area which serves as vehicular distribution and a short-term car parking area.

Volumetrically the new buildings are identical to their neighbours. However, the residential tower differs from its neighbours in offering clearly oriented flat layouts by zoning the spaces in a north-south direction. Hence the south facade is also designed to be inhabited: a single openable glass skin protects a second light and insulated wall. The space between these walls and its material characteristics are dependent on its use. Sometimes wintergarden, sometimes kitchen, ultimately the design of this element is left to the tenants.

The office tower is a building with an intelligent skin. The facade regulates temperature and ventilation and allows the control of daylight. The primary structure serves as an air duct and provides thermal mass.

diagramm raumstruktur
diagram of urban fabric

78

modell, blick von süden
model, looking north

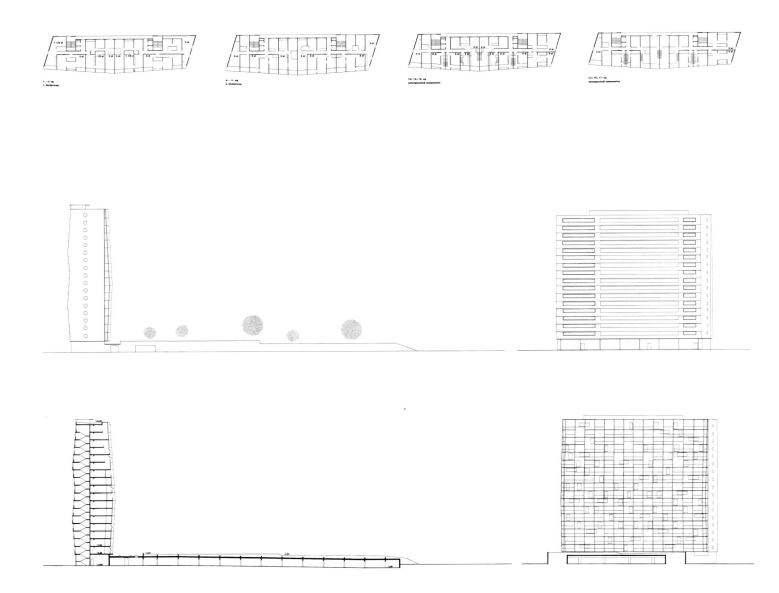

grundrisse und schnitte wohnhaus
plans and sections of apartment house

grundrisse und schnitte bürogebäude
plans and sections of office building

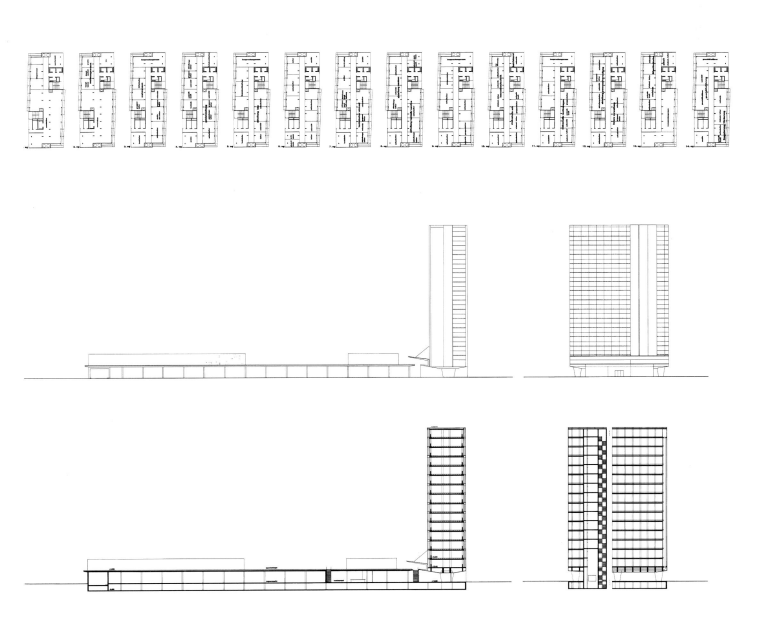

modell, blick von westen
model, looking east

WBG Marzahn

bebauung südufer maselakekanal · development southbank maselakekanal · 1994

aufgabe
Entwurf eines Wohnquartiers in der
neuen Wasserstadt Spandau
umfang
ca. 200 ha
standort
Grundstück am Maselakekanal zwischen der
noch zu errichtenden "Nordbrücke" und einem
bestehenden Gewerbebetrieb

brief
*Masterplan for a residential quarter within
the newly founded "Wasserstadt" Spandau*
size
approx. 200 acr.
site
*Between a bridge (which is yet to be
constructed), a canal and an existing factory*

Wohnen am Kanal bedeutete für uns maxima-
ler Kontakt zum Wasser, den das als Schema
vorgegebene Muster von Block und Straße
nicht zu geben imstande schien.

Da die Blockstruktur aus dem Wunsch nach
Minimierung der überbauten Flächen entstanden war, galt es nachzuweisen, daß eine
offenere Bebauung nicht zu Lasten der Außen-
räume gehen würde. Eine Untersuchung im
"Künstlichen Himmel" zeigte, daß ein Auf-
brechen der vorgegebenen Struktur bei gleich-
bleibender Dichte machbar und sinnvoll ist.
Der Besonnung folgend und unter Ausgren-
zung der Schallbelästigung von Hauptstraße
und Gewerbebetrieb wurde so das Gelände
rechtwinklig zum Kanal in Garten- und
Straßenbereiche aufgeteilt.

Die Forderung nach Freihaltung der Straßen
vom ruhenden Verkehr und nach Minimierung
des Gründungsaufwandes der Gebäude in
schwierigem Baugrund führte darüberhinaus
zu einer horizontalen Trennung des Geländes
in andienende und Wohn-Geschoße.

*Living by the water meant for us a maximum
contact with this element, a quality which the
given scheme of block and street wasn't able
to provide.*

*As the block structure came from a desire to
minimise the footprint of the buildings, it was
for us to prove that we wouldn't open up the
fabric at the expense of surrounding outside
areas. However, a simulation in an artificial
sky showed that the opening of the blocks
(despite equal density) seemed practical and
sensible. Following the sun and trying to
avoid noise pollution from the main street and
the adjacent factory, the site was divided into
street and garden spaces.*

*The requirement for streets without parking
and the necessity to save on foundations in
difficult ground conditions led to a horizontal
layering of the site into serving and served
floors. Car park floors are located underneath
the garden areas, so that there is a clear
separation between these and the streets by
virtue of a level change.*

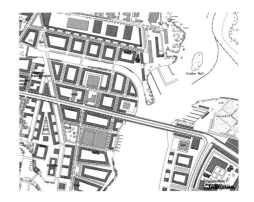

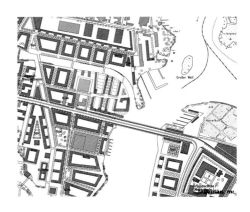

masterplan (vorgabe)
master plan (given)

lageplan (vorschlag)
site plan (proposal)

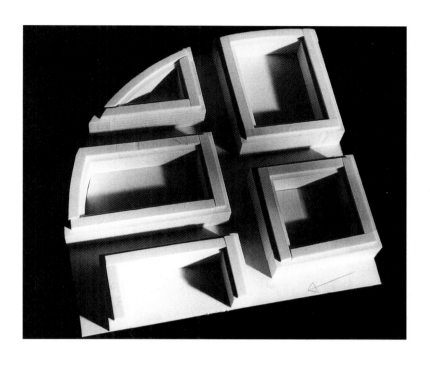

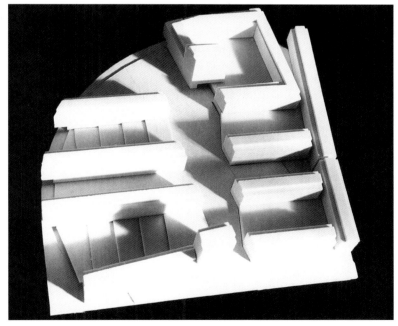

vergleichende besonnungsstudien
vorgabe
entwurf

comparative solar studies
given
proposal

bebauung südufer maselakekanal
development southbank
maselakekanal
1994

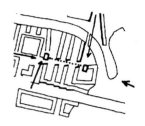

Als Folge dieser Maßnahme sind Garten- von Straßenbereichen durch einen Höhensprung getrennt; was einen markanten proportionalen Unterschied zwischen dem Querschnitt der öffentlichen Straßen und dem der privaten Gartenzonen zur Folge hat.

Die unterschiedliche räumliche Qualität der beiden Bereiche wird durch die differenzierte Behandlung der Fassaden unterstützt: Straßenfassaden sind flach und massiv, Gartenfassaden skulptural und gläsern gehalten.

Über die rationale Zonierung der Bebauung hinweg formen räumliche und volumetrische Betonungen ein System von Blickräumen und -beziehungen, die den Gesamtbereich beleben und kompositorisch zusammenbinden.

However, this "parking plinth" also produces a significant proportional difference in the section between that of the (lower) garden as compared to that of the (taller) street areas.

This spatial difference is reinforced by a different treatment of the façades, those of the street are flat and solid, while those of the garden are sculptural and translucent.

Across this rational site layout a system of volumetric and spatial highlights tie the whole quarter into a varied and interesting composition.

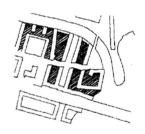

boulevard
blickachsen · *view points*
gartenhöfe · *gardens*
öffnung zum wasser · *opening to the water*

perspektive boulevard
boulevard perspective

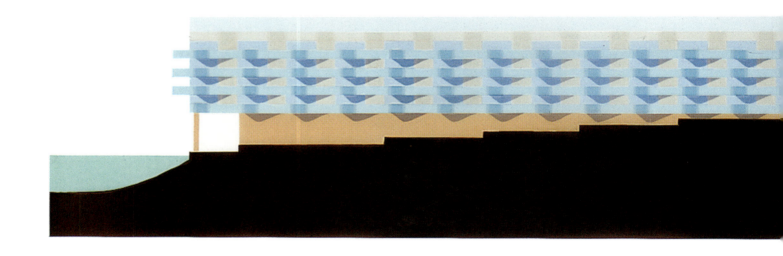

ansicht straßenraum
elevation street

ansicht gartenraum
elevation garden

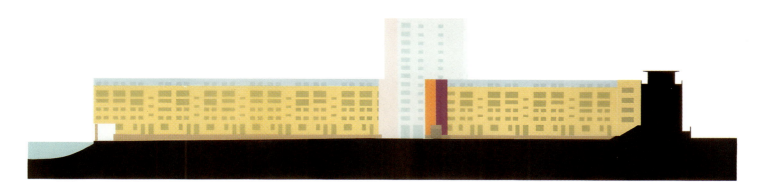

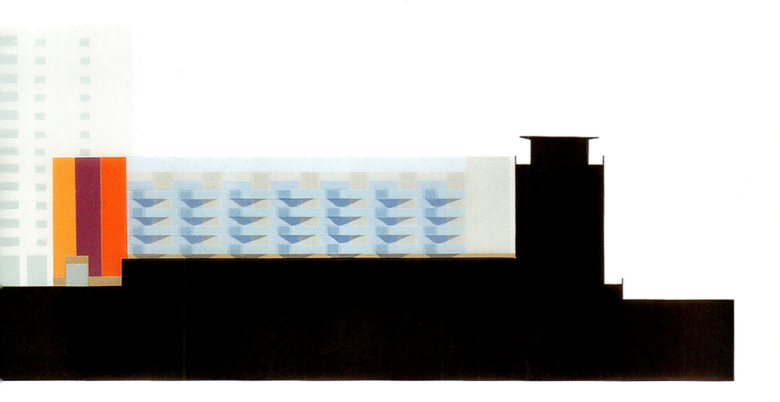

perspektive piazza
piazza perspective

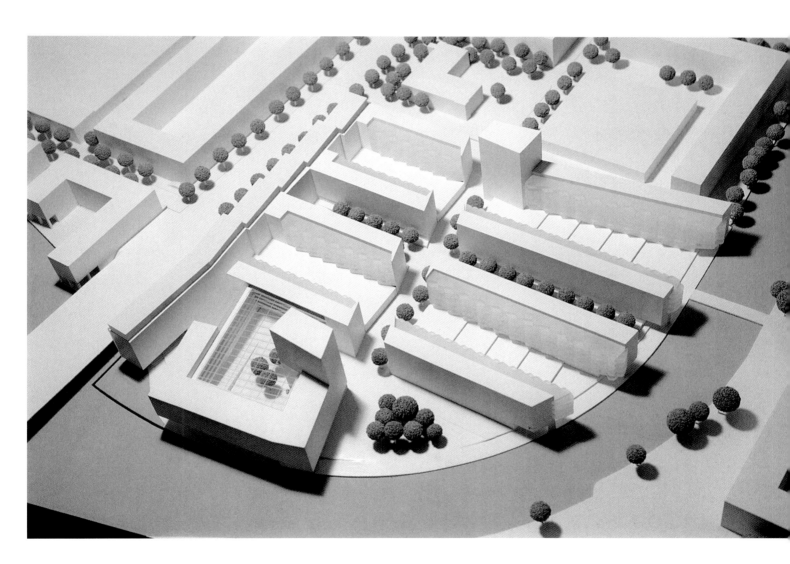

modell
model

jüdische schule · jewish school · 1990

jüdische schule
jewish school
1990

aufgabe
Neubau einer Grundschule für die
jüdische Gemeinde in Berlin
umfang
6.800 m^2
standort
Ein Villenquartier am Rande des
Grunewalds in Berlin-Charlottenburg

brief
Primary school for the
Jewish community in Berlin
size
6.800 m^2
site
Residential district at the edge of the
Grunewald Forest in Charlottenburg

Das Wettbewerbsgrundstück am Rande des
Grunewalds könnte man als ein Stück Land in
der Stadt beschreiben; und während die
"grünen" Eigenschaften dieses Ortes Schule
und Schülern zugute kommen sollen, will man
die für ein so zentrales Grundstück seltene
Flora und Fauna vor "der Stadt" schützen.

Als Lösung dieses Konfliktes etabliert der
Entwurf ein "zweites Grundstück" über dem
Waldboden. Ein Stück künstlicher Landschaft
mit vielfachem Nutzen wie beispielsweise
Sonnendeck, überschaubare Spielfläche,
sichere Insel im "dunklen Wald".

Über und unter diesem Deck entstehen, wie
von selbst, Territorien von "Zelt" und "Höhle".
So sind die Klassenräume in den oberen
Geschossen in einem einfachen, leicht kon-
struierten Glaskörper untergebracht, der den
Unterricht inmitten der Kronen von hohen
Kiefernbäumen stattfinden läßt.

The site into which a school is to be inserted
is like a small piece of countryside in the city.
Its qualities are to be made available to the
pupils, yet at the same time its flora and
fauna (rare for such a central location) are to
be preserved.

To resolve this conflict the scheme proposes
a second site raised above the ground. As a
piece of artificial nature it offers a variety of
uses: sundeck, protected playspace, a safe
haven in the dark forest.

This deck also divides the section of the build-
ing into the territories of "tent" and "cave".
Above the deck, classrooms are accommo-
dated amongst the branches of tall pine trees
in a light structure of steel and glass. Below
the deck most of the group facilities such as
the theatre, dining room, gymnasium etc. are
located in spaces cast into the forest ground.

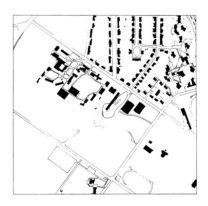

photo wettbewerbsgelände
site photograph

Dagegen liegen alle Gemeinschaftseinrich-
tungen wie Theatersaal, Mensa, Turnhalle etc.
unter dem "fliegenden" Garten eingefügt in die
(künstliche) Erde.

Das Gebäude faßt zwei Erlebniswelten in
einem Komplex zusammen: den skulptural
geformten, dramatisch beleuchteten Waldboden und die lichte Welt darüber auf einem
"arkadischen Teppich".

Stadt und Landschaft, "Natur" und Künstlich-
keit wechseln einander ab, übernehmen die
gegenseitigen Rollen – bilden ein hybrides
Raumgefüge dialektischer Natur.

*So the building embraces two worlds: the
communal places (predominantly nurturing
the body) inhabit a sensuous nether landscape where the rooms are foot-printed into
the forest floor and the more fluid circulation
spaces following the ramped earth coalesce
between these rooms and their negative
counterparts – large glass "vases" bearing
light down to the forest depths. By contrast,
those rooms for education of the mind enjoy
the ambient light and views at leaf-level,
housed in a rectilinear clearly "city"-devel-
oped building.*

*City and countryside, Nature and Artifice
complement each other, play each other's
rôles and combine to form a hybrid whole
of a dialectic nature.*

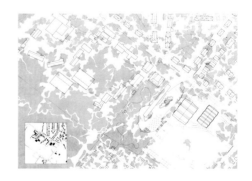

situation
location plan

lageplan
site plan

WALDSCHULALLEE

MARIENBURGER ALLEE

NARBIGSTRASSE

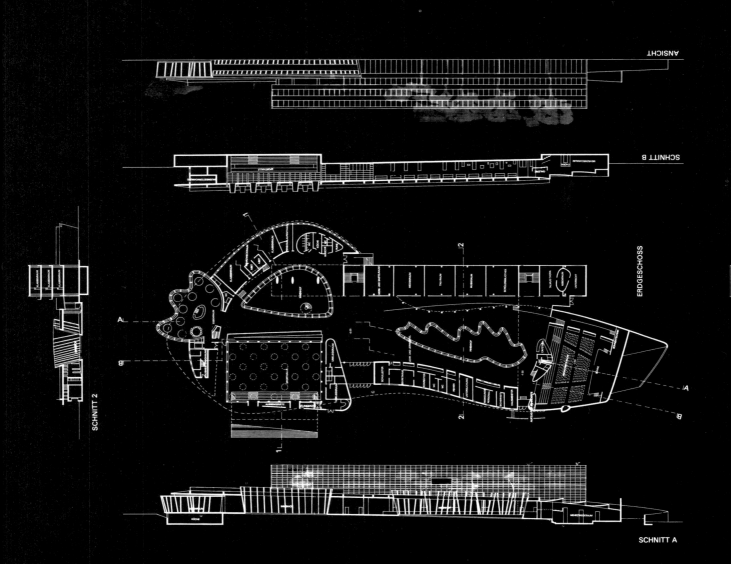

ANSICHT

SCHNITT B

ERDGESCHOSS

SCHNITT 2

SCHNITT A

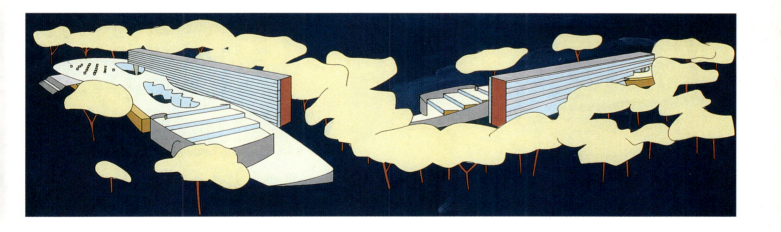

grundriß erdgeschoß/schnitte
ground floor plan/sections

perspektivskizze
sketch perspective

101

innenraum
below the deck

blick von der straße
view from the street

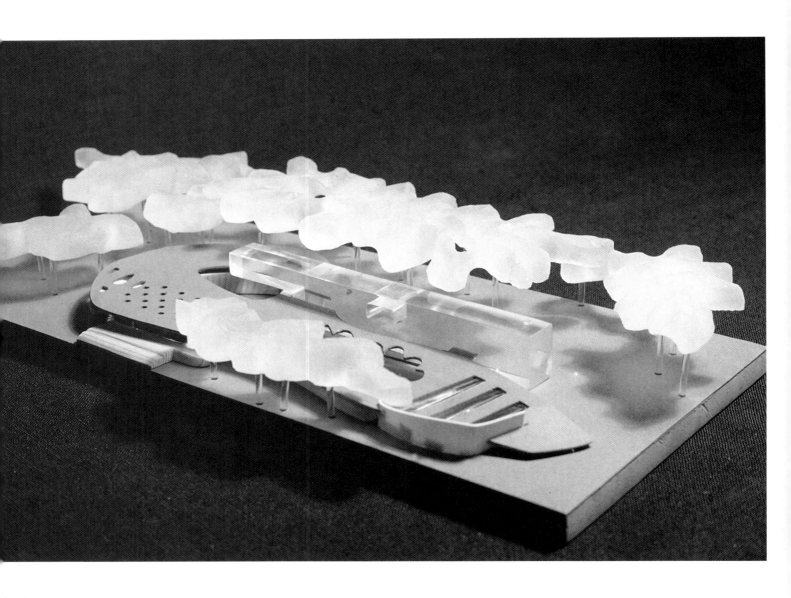

modell
model

gebäudeteile
composite parts

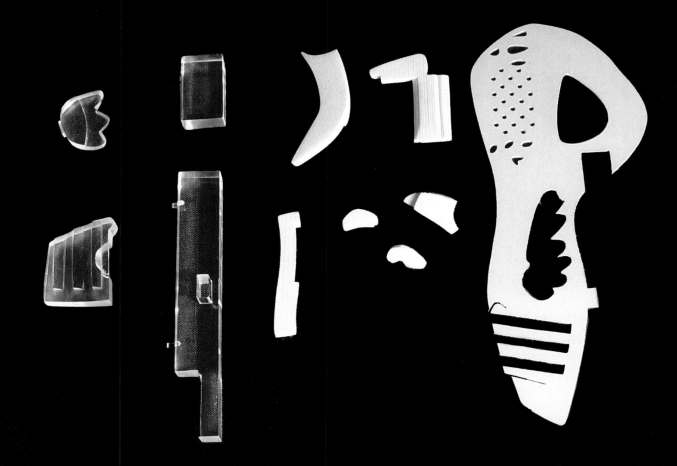

deutscher bundestag eisenblock · 1994

deutscher bundestag alsenblock
1994

aufgabe
Verwaltungsgebäude für die Mitglieder
des Deutschen Bundestages in Berlin
fläche
ca. 120.000 m² Büros, Seminarräume,
Ausschußsäle etc.
standort
Teil des neuen Regierungsviertels
nördlich des Reichstagsgebäudes

brief
*Administration building for the members
of the German Parliament in Berlin*
size
*approx. 120,000 m² offices,
meeting facilities, chambers etc.*
site
*Part of the new governmental
area north of the Reichstag*

Die städtebauliche Vorgabe des "Regierungs-
gebäudes" verlangte eine volumetrische
Disziplin, der wir uns nicht entziehen wollten.
Ausgangspunkt unseres Entwurfsprozeßes war
das vorgegebene Gebäudevolumen von 120 m
Breite, 240 m Länge und 24 m Höhe.

Das letztlich resultierende Gebäude entstand
aus einer Serie von Unterteilungen, Perfora-
tionen und Artikulationen dieses vorgegebenen
Blocks.

Zwei Qualitäten machen die Besonderheiten
des Entwurfes aus: zum einen wird der riesige
Block durch die Gestaltung der Fassade ent-
"materialisiert", zum anderen wird dies
scheinbar monolithische Erscheinungsbild des
Körpers durch artikulierte Vielfalt der inneren
Organisation kontrastiert.

Seine drei Atrien lassen das Gebäude wie ein
einziges Volumen mit drei "Fenstern" erschei-
nen. Der massive Bereich der Fassade besteht
aus vier gleichen horizontalen Bändern pro
Geschoß. Zwei Bänder aus Glas, eins aus
Klinker, eins aus einer Überlagerung beider
Materialien. Die Atrien sind mit einem Schleier
aus Glas geschlossen.

*In acceptance of the masterplan for the new
governmental area, the starting point for the
design of this building was a solid envelope
measuring 120 x 240 x 24 m.*

*The new building's character and identity is
achieved by the material treatment of its exterior on the one hand, and the spatial rich-
ness and variety of its interior on the other.*

*Two qualities are significant for the design:
through the form of the facade the gigantic
block is dematerialized. At the same time the
seemingly monolithic appearance of the
building is contrasted with an articulate
variety of inner organisation.*

*With its three atria the building appears as
one continuous solid mass with large win-
dows cut into it. These atria are covered in
minimal glass skins veiling the bustle of the
building's interior, and reinforcing a calm to
the exterior. In the „solid" section the facade
is subdivided into four equal horizontal bands
per floor. Two bands are made of glass, one is
made of brick, and the other one is formed
through the overlap of both materials.*

masterplan spreebogen

lageplan
site plan

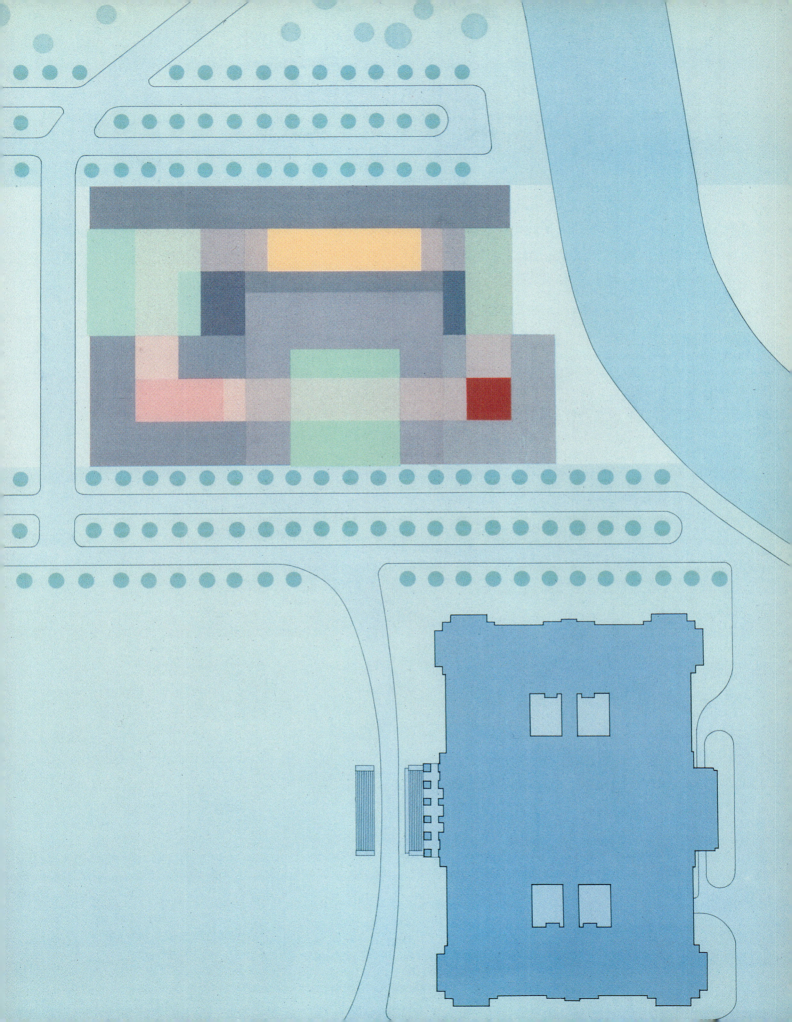

Die transparente/transluzente Materialität des
Gebäudes und die bewußt zweideutige
Maßstäblichkeit geben ihm subtile Distanz zum
wilhelminischen Pomp des Reichstags.

Im Innern verbindet ein sanft ansteigender
Rundweg die drei Atrien und drei weitere Höfe,
der als Haupterschließungs- und Orien-
tierungsroute dient. Er führt den Benutzer
durch ein Gebäude, das in seiner sinnlichen
Erlebnisvielfalt mit dem Weg durch ein kleines
Stadtquartier verglichen werden könnte.

*This transparent/translucent skin deliberately
gives the building an ambiguity of scale and
physicality, whose presence is subtle in clear
contrast to the Wilhelminian pomp of the
Reichstag.*

*In the interior the atria and three additional
courtyards are connected by a wide and gent-
ly rising route which serves as the main
access and orientation for the building. It
leads through a sequence of spaces which,
with their spatial variety and sensual rich-
ness, could be compared to a route through a
small city quarter.*

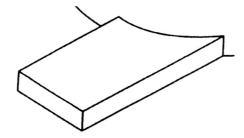

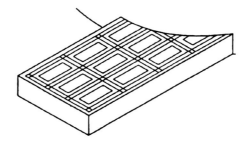

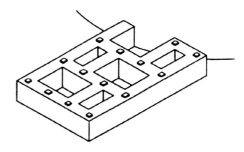

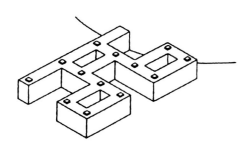

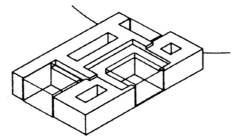

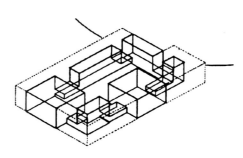

vorgegebenes volumen
given volume

büroraster
office grid

ausrichtung auf die spree
response to the river

interne + externe höfe
internal + external courtyards

atrien als schaufenster
atria as showcases

verbindender rundweg
connecting route

eingangshalle
entrance hall

bürohof
office court-yard

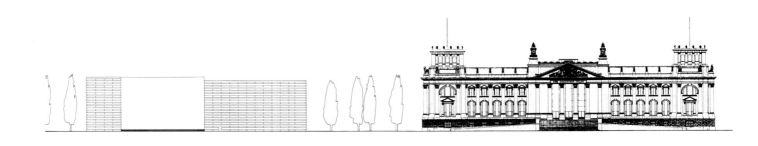

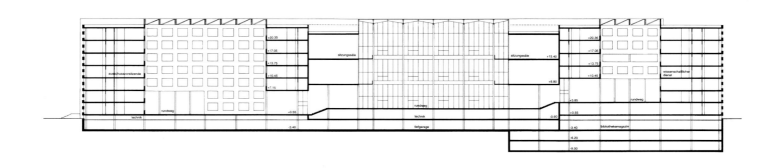

westansicht
west elevation

längsschnitt
longitudinal section

grundriß ebene 5
plan at level 5

114

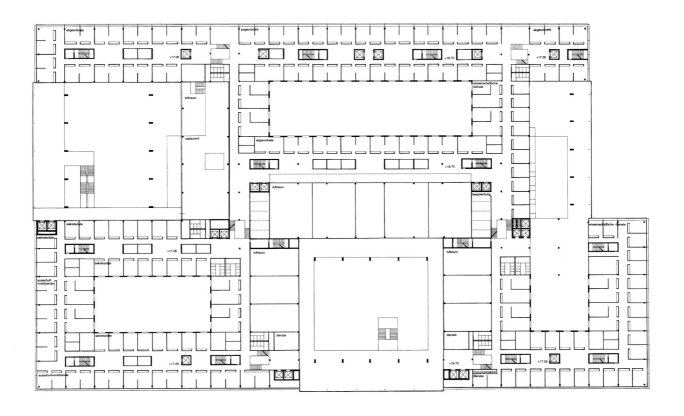

115

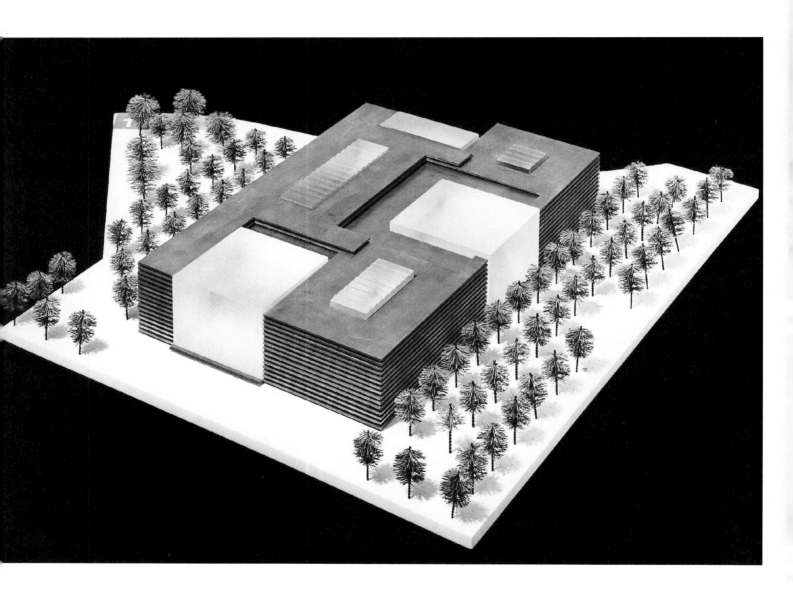

modell
model

116

bundespräsidialamt · 1994

bundespräsidialamt
1994

aufgabe
Verwaltungsgebäude des deutschen
Bundespräsidenten in Berlin
fläche
ca. 8.000 m^2 Büro- und Sitzungsräume
mit entsprechenden Nebennutzungen
standort
Grundstück neben Schloß Bellevue
(Amts- und Wohnsitz des Präsidenten)
im Tiergarten

brief
*Administration building for
the German President*
area
*approx. 8,000 m^2 office and meeting spaces,
with their respective ancillary facilities.*
site
*Adjacent to Schloss Bellevue
(the President's residence)
in the Tiergarten*

Zum einen schien uns die Aufgabe die intelli-
gente Plazierung des neuen Baukörpers in die
besondere städtebauliche Situation des Tiergartens zu erfordern. Darüberhinaus geht das
Gebäude als Filter und "Manipulator" seines
Umgebungsklimas eine neue Symbiose mit
seiner natürlichen Umgebung ein.

Abweichend von den Empfehlungen der Wett-
bewerbsausschreibung wählten wir für das
neue Verwaltungsgebäude des Bundespräsidenten in Berlin ein Rest- anstelle des vorge-
schlagenen "Filet"-Stücks: nämlich ein Dreieck
zwischen Straße, Präsidentengarten und der
Vorfahrt zum Schloß Bellevue, um die "Privatisierung" weiterer öffentlichen Flächen des so
stark benutzten Tiergartens zu vermeiden.

Darüberhinaus schien es uns nicht unange-
messen, das Amtsgebäude des Präsidenten
vom öffentlichen Raum deutlich sichtbar zu
lassen, anstatt es im Park zu verstecken.
In der Geometrie des Tiergartens bietet die
Einfügung des Gebäudes an dieser Stelle
quasi retroaktiv einen Grund für die Abwei-
chung der Straße vom geraden Strahl des
"Großen Sterns" (die tatsächlich historisch
auf komplizierte Grundstücksverhältnisse
zurückzuführen ist).

*For us the scheme seemed to require an
intelligent integration of the new building
volume into the particular situation of the
park. In addition, responding to its natural
surroundings – the design attempts to re-
define the building envelope as a filter and
manipulator of the environment.*

*Deviating from the recommendations of the
competition brief, we chose to locate the
President's administration on a redundant
rather than a prime site: the triangular piece
of land between the street, the President's
garden and the castle's approach instead of
the much frequented adjacent parkland.*

*The insertion of the building at this point
retroactively provides a raison d'être for the
geometry of the situation, and allows for the
construction of the sizeable complex without
further occupation of park land which to date
has been public.*
*Therefore, as opposed to the hidden pavilion
suggested by the brief, this location also
permits the experience of the President's
presence in the city.*
*The bushes and trees occupying the site now
would be replaced by a building edge which –
with its layers of skins – would present the
spatial and pictorial quality of the forest edge.*

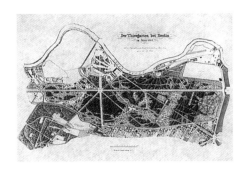

tiergarten 1833
tiergarten 1994

luftaufnahme des wettbewerbsgeländes
aerial view of the site

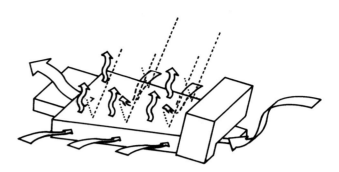

Das Gebäude selbst vereint in sich die Aspekte von "Haus" und "Garten": Ein Steinhaus wird von einer Glashaut umhüllt. Nutzungs- und Aufenthaltsräume befinden sich in und zwischen diesen Schichten. Im Gegensatz zur pointierten Frontalität des Schloßes sind hier die Gebäudeoberflächen, die Innen von Außen trennen, keine "Fassaden", sondern Häute, die Wärme, Licht, Luft, Schall und Wind filtern, um sie vom Gebäude fernzuhalten oder ins Gebäude einzulassen. Sie bilden Raumkanten sich überlagernder Hüllen unterschiedlicher Transparenz und Reflektivität, die die Qualität des "Waldrands" haben. Der höhere Gebäudeteil dient als "Windschaufel", die (insbesondere im Sommer) über den Bäumen Wind "einfängt", um den Hauptraum des Gebäudes mit einer Sommerbrise zu durchlüften.

The building itself combines the aspects of "house" and "garden". A stone building is enclosed by a glass volume. The areas of use are located in and between these two territories. In contrast to the pointed frontality of the "Schloss", the surfaces which divide the interior from the exterior are not facades but skins which filter heat, light, air, sound and wind, using the natural conditions to the best advantage of the building's internal and external environment.

haus als filter
building envelope as filter

lageplan
site plan

SPREEWEG

STRASSE DES 17.JUNI

GROSSER STERN

außenperspektive
exterior perspective

124

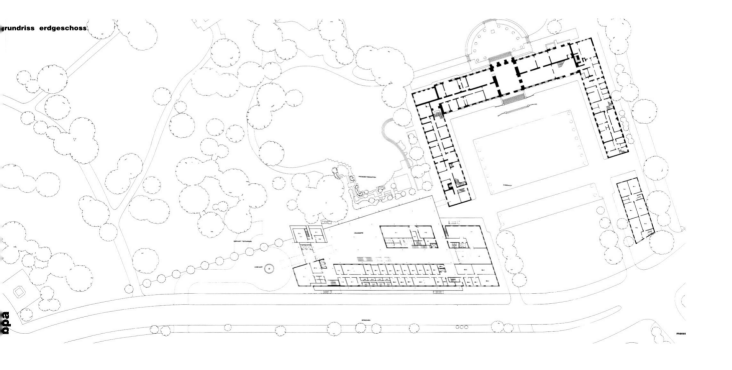

grundriß erdgeschoß
ground floor plan

innenperspektive
interior perspective

modell

model

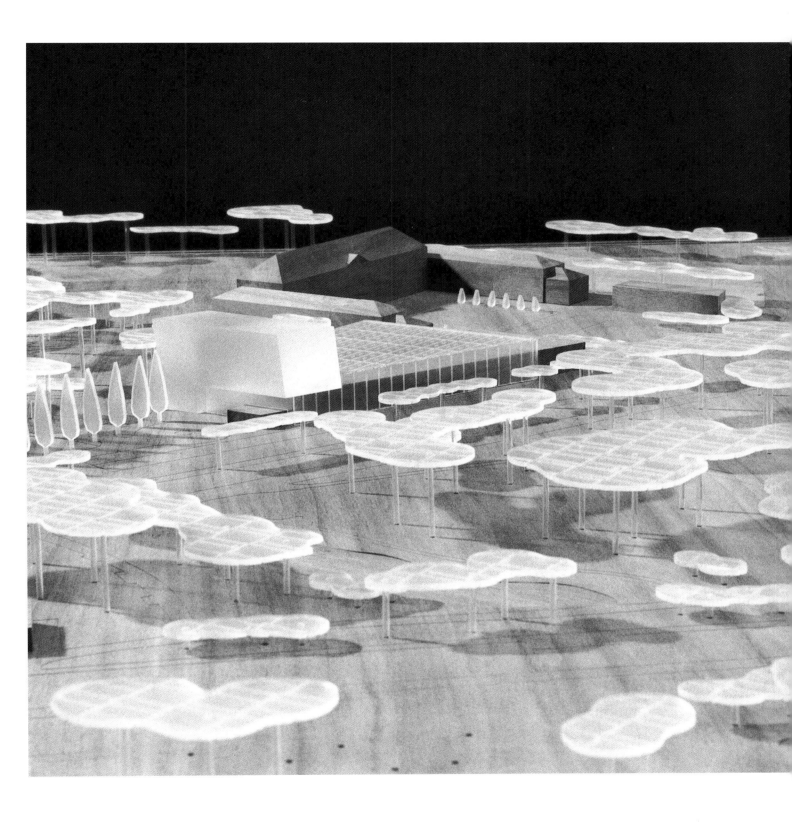

innovationszentrum photonik · centre for innovation in photonics · 1995/96

innovationszentrum photonik
centre for innovation in photonics
1995/96

aufgabe
Gewerbebau für Mietflächen, mit einer
Größe von 100 m^2 - 1000 m^2, für Büros, Labore,
Werk- und Produktionsstätten
umfang
ca. 11.000 m^2
standort
Wissenschaftstandort Adlershof, einem
neuen Gewerbe- und Wissenschaftspark
am ehemaligen Flughafen Johannisthal

brief
Multifunctional Building with lettable
units of 100 - 1000 m^2 for workshops,
production facilities, laboratories and offices
size
approx. 11.000 m^2
site
"Wissenschaftstandort Adlershof", a new
business and science park near the former
airport of Johannisthal

Das Projekt ist in erster Linie aus den
funktional-technischen Anforderungen an die
Gebäude entstanden: Der Wunsch nach
Minimierung des Erschließungsaufwandes und
die Forderung nach großflächigen Dunkelzonen
(für optische Labore) führte zu drei Gebäuden,
deren tiefer Grundriß über ein zentrales
Rückgrat erschlossen wird. Einzelne
Nutzeinheiten werden dann im rechten Winkel
zu diesem Rückgrat von der Geschoßfläche
abgetrennt. Aufgrund der Forderung nach
Flächengrößen von 100 bis 1000 m^2 entstehen
zwangsläufig unterschiedliche Gebäudetiefen,
die hier genutzt wurden, um dem Gesamt-
körper weiche Konturen zu geben, was
wiederum das problemlose Einfügen der
neuen Gebäude in die bestehende Bebauung
erleichtert.

Die drei internen Erschließungslinien der drei
neuen Bauten verbinden jeweils Eingänge an
den wichtigen Straßen am Perimeter des
Bereiches und einen als "Focus" bezeichneten
Mittelpunkt, der alle Gebäude des Photonik-
zentrums miteinander verbindet.

The brief asked for three buildings, housing
the above-mentioned facilities, to be sited
amongst existing buildings, streets and exter-
nal spaces of assorted provenance and qual-
ity. The site is bounded to the south by the
open space of the so-called "lens", and to the
north and west by existing and new roads
repectively.

We felt that the situation by the "lens", in
particular, where the three former Academy
buildings form a coherent space of gentle
scale (they are each three stories, with half
a storey being sunk into the ground) demand-
ed other than the imposition of yet more recti-
linear blocks – the new buildings of the Photo-
nics Centre should be legible as another set of
free-standing objects.

The "soft" contours of the new buildings suc-
ceed in giving the ensemble an identity, and
at the same time they do not deny the
strength of the existing context in their ad-
mission of free-flowing space. They also posi-
tively respond to the impressive groups of
mature trees near the existing buildings to
the southeast of the site.

schwarzplan
figure-ground plan

lageplan
site plan

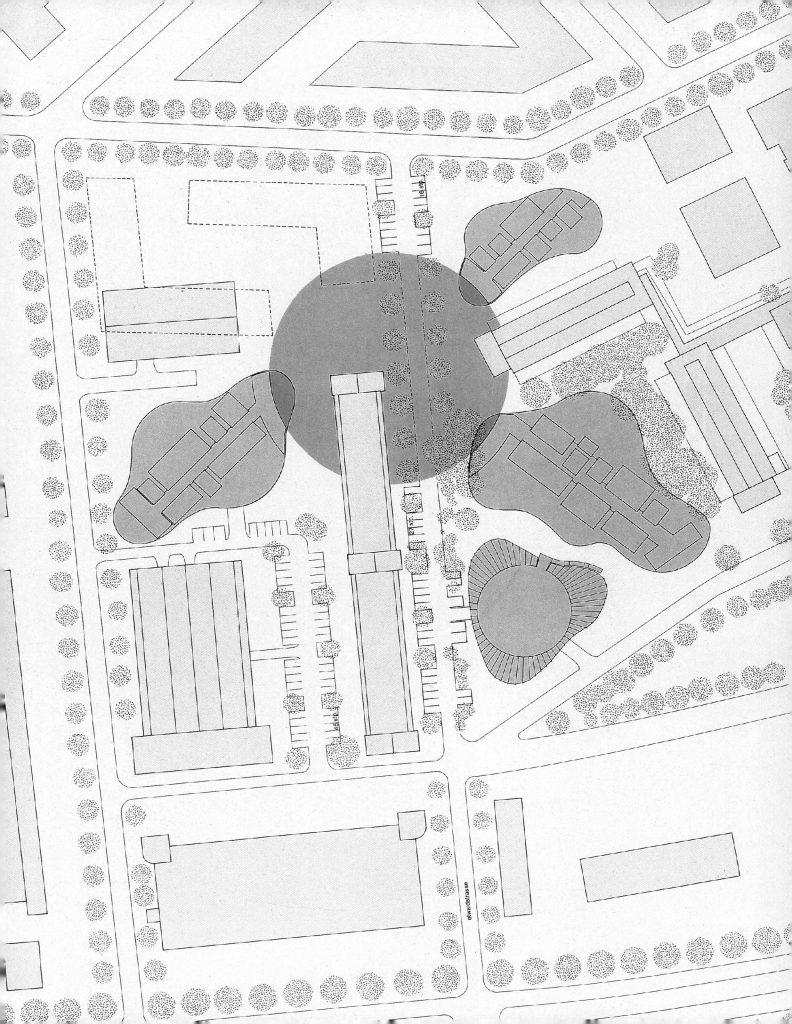

Im ersten Bauabschnitt wurde darüberhinaus vorgeschlagen, Flächen für die Produktion in einer von den Laboren und Büros getrennten Halle unterzubringen.
Die Gebäude selbst sind als Betonfertigteil-konstruktionen geplant, die die Integration der gesamten Haustechnik in dem Maß erlaubt, daß jeder Punkt innerhalb der geplanten Flächen ohne Zusatzaufwand sowohl von oben als auch von unten durch Technik "angefahren" werden kann.

Die Fassade ist als zweischalige Klimafassade geplant. Die zwischen den Schichten liegenden Sonnenschutzpaneele bestimmen das Er-scheinungsbild des Gebäudes: Ihre Farbe folgt um den Gebäudekörper herum dem Farb-spektrum des Lichts.

The development of the buildings themselves mostly followed from the requirements of the brief. The necessity of minimal circulation and the requirement for large zones without day-light (for optical laboratories) lead to three buildings with comparatively deep plans organised around central access and service spines. Individual units are laid out at right angles to this central corridor. The undulating path of the facades result in varying depths of the buildings, which are used to advantage to create lettable units of different sizes.

Each circulation spine connects two entrances, one of which is directed to an important street at the perimeter of the site, and the other of which is pinned to the so-called "Focus" which connects all buildings of the "Photonics Centre".

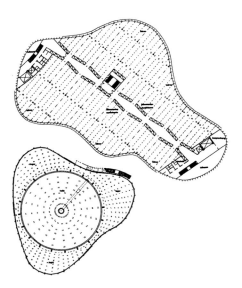

grundriß
plan

perspektive
perspective

ansicht
elevation

modell
model

138

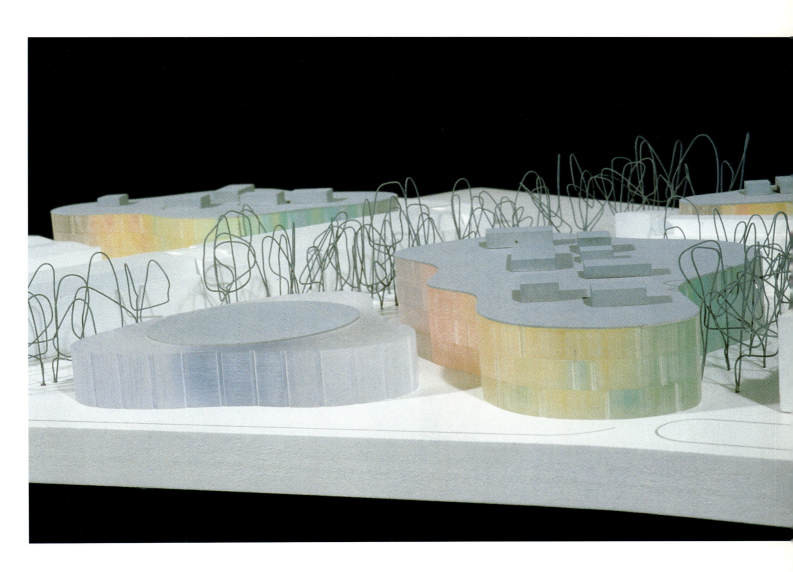

	born 1957		geboren 1955
85	Diploma at the Architectural Associa-tion School of Architecture, London	84	Diplome an der Hochschule der Künste, Berlin und an der Architectural Association, School of Architecture, London
84-87	Worked with A & P Smithson on the School of Architecture and Engineering, Bath	84-88	Mitglied des Office for Metropolitan Architecture (OMA), London
87-90	Teaching at Croydon College of Art and at the AA, London	85-90	Unit Master an der AA, London
88	Office with matthias sauerbruch	88	Büro mit louisa hutton

Visiting critic at various universities in Europe and Canada

Zu Gast an zahlreichen Universitäten in Europa und Canada

robert harbison

Robert Harbison was born in Baltimore and
lives in London. He teaches at the University of
North London and the Architectural
Association and is the author of numerous
books, among them – Eccentric spaces,
Deliberate Regression: "Primitivism from
Jean-Jacques Rousseau to Kandinsky", and
"The Built, the Unbuilt and the Unbuildable"
(published in German by Birkhäuser).

werkverzeichnis/works

88

IBA-Projekt "Wohnhaus am Checkpoint Charlie", Berlin	+	in Partnerschaft mit Elia Zenghelis dirk alten, reni keller, eleni gigantes, barbara burren, alex wall
	structure	Polonyi und Fink, Berlin Roscher und Fast, Berlin
	services	Büro Baller, Berlin
Lützowplatz, Platzgestaltung, Berlin (competition)	land	Diana Bell, London
Institut für Anatomie, Berlin (competition)		
Exhibition Royal Academy of Arts at ICAF 88	+	ashley hicks
Nairac House, London	+	hilke rackow
	structure	Dewhurst Macfarlane, London
"Metropolitan Park", Project for the Metamorphosis of the "Westhafen"area, Berlin	+	anna könig
	structure	Dewhurst Macfarlane, London
"Completion instead of Demolition", Polemic for the Conservation of Paternoster Square, London	+	heike metzger

89

Office Interior, Notting Hill, London	structure	Dewhurst Macfarlane, London
Sellar House, Kensington, London	structure	Dewhurst Macfarlane, London
Stebbings House, Barnsbury, London	structure	Dewhurst Macfarlane, London
	quantities	Andrew Turner, London
Junction Building, Birmingham (competition)	structure	Dewhurst Macfarlane, London
	services	Fulcrum, London
Tokyo International Forum (competition)	+	tom cary, eddy chui, ebba zernack, susanne isa
	structure	Dewhurst Macfarlane, London
	services	Robert Scott, London
Milan Office of the Future (competition)	+	megan williams

werkverzeichnis/works

90

SH House, Notting Hill, London	structure	Dewhurst Macfarlane, London
	quantities	Andrew Turner, London
Johnson Flat, Holland Park, London	structure	Dewhurst Macfarlane, London
GSW-Hauptverwaltung, Kreuzberg, Berlin	comp	juan lucas young, simon hart,
(invited competition, due to be completed in 98)		nicola murphy, nicholas boyarsky,
		liz adams
	design	juan lucas young, brian lilley,
		harvey langston-jones, brenda webster,
		susanne hofmann, karl-friedrich
		hörnlein, anne-françoise chollet
	working	juan lucas young, anna bader-hardt,
	drawings	michail blösser, philip engelbrecht,
		iman ghazali, heinz jirout
		brian lilley, stefan wirth, felix held,
		jens ludloff, govert gerritsen, christian
		galvão, jeff kirby, francis henderson,
		klaus de winder, moritz theden
	model 1	juan lucas young
	model 2	Monath + Menzel, Berlin
		Hamlyn Terry
	model 3	fredrik källström
	structure	Ove Arup + Partners, Arup GmbH
	services	Ove Arup + Partners, Arup GmbH
	site	Harms + Partner, Berlin
Wohnpark, Bottrop,	+	heike metzger, stefan mang, chaz piggot
(competition)	structure	Dewhurst Macfarlane, London
	land	Freie Planungsgruppe, Berlin
Jüdische Grundschule, Berlin	+	juan lucas young, ceso carena,
(competition)		kenneth ross, dorrien hopley
	structure	Dewhurst Macfarlane, London
"Corporeal Gardens", a Public Building for London	+	juan lucas young
	structure	Dewhurst Macfarlane, London

91

Hauptpumpwerk, Wilmersdorf,	+	juan lucas young
(invited competition)	structure	Dewhurst Macfarlane, London
"Block 109", Friedrichstadt, Berlin	+	brian lilley, juan lucas young, renée tobe,
(invited competition)		harvey langston-jones, lia kanagini,
		cara bamford
	structure	Ove Arup + Partners, London
	model	alec vassiliades

92

Bürobebauung "Wilhelmsruher Damm",	+	juan lucas young, harvey langston-jones,
(invited competition)		brian lilley, lia kanagini
	services	Ove Arup + Partners, London
	model	Unit 22, London

werkverzeichnis/works

Olympische Schwimm- und Radsporthallen, Berlin (competition)	+	juan lucas young, harvey langston-jones
	structure	Dewhurst Macfarlane, London
	services	Max Fordham, London
	model	Unit 22, London

93

Kulturzentrum, Konstanz (invited competition)	+	brenda webster, andrew shields, anthony hoete, miwako nakamura
	structure	Dewhurst Macfarlane, London
	model	alec vassiliades

"Heinrich Heine Strasse", Luisenstadt, Berlin (competition for masterplan)	+	simon hart, brenda webster, miwako nakamura, anthony hoete

Europan 3, Rummelsburger Bucht, Berlin (competition)	+	juan lucas young, susanne hofmann, brian lilley

House, Kensington, London	+	simon hart, anthony hoete
	structure	Dewhurst Macfarlane, London
	quantities	Andrew Turner, London

94

Stadtmitte Marzahn, Berlin (invited competition for masterplan)	+	bettina vismann, gordon black, susanne hofmann, brian lilley, juan lucas young
	land	B+B, Amsterdam, Bram Breetveld
	model	Network Modelmakers, London
	traffic	Arup GmbH, Berlin

Deutsches Bibliotheksinstitut, Berlin (competition)	+	brian lilley, juan lucas young

Bundespräsidialamt, Berlin (competition)	+	frank chui, julia neubauer, brian lilley, juliet searight
	structure	Dewhurst Macfarlane, London
	services	Arup GmbH
	model	Monath + Menzel, Berlin

Wohnbebauung Wasserstadt, Berlin (invited competition)	+	holger kleine, vera gloor, julia neubauer, frank chui, felix held
	traffic	Arup GmbH
	model	Monath + Menzel, Berlin

Deutscher Bundestag (Alsenblock), Berlin (competition)	+	vera gloor, katja rohrbach, felix held, holger kleine
	services	Arup GmbH
	model	Monath + Menzel, Berlin, Hamlyn Terry

Hauptverwaltung der Wohnbaugesellschaft Marzahn, Berlin (invited competition)	+	felix held, birgit hirschmann, holger kleine
	model	Monath + Menzel, Berlin birgit hirschmann

werkverzeichnis/works

H House, London	+	simon hart, project architect
	structure	Dewhurst Macfarlane, London
	quantities	Andrew Turner, London
Wohnungsbau Hohenschönhausen,	+	holger kleine, francis henderson,
35 Wohnungen		katja rohrbach, frank chiu
95		
Felix Nussbaum Museum, Osnabrück	+	vera gloor, katja rohrbach
(competition)		francis henderson, holger kleine
	services	Arup GmbH, Berlin
	model	fredrik källström
		Monath + Menzel, Berlin
Innovationszentrum Photonik, Berlin	comp	holger frielingsdorf, katja rohrbach,
(invited competition, due to be completed 98)		francis henderson,
	design	klaus de winder, holger frielingsdorf,
		kirsten siepmann, markus pfändler,
		amir rothkegel, annikka meier,
		camilla wilkinson
	model	fredrik källström
	structure	Krebs + Kiefer, Berlin
	services	Zibell, Willner + Partner, Köln
	site	Harms + Partner, Berlin
Bürogebäude, Spittelmarkt, Berlin	+	laurent touray, andreas veauthier,
(invited competition)		francis henderson, felix jourdan,
		kirsten siepmann
	structure	Arup GmbH, Berlin
	model	Müller + Hauel, Berlin
Konzerthalle für Bremen	+	holger kleine, laurent touray,
(invited competition)		andreas veauthier, francis henderson,
		kirsten siepmann, annikka meier,
		felix jourdan
	structure	Ove Arup + Partners, London
	services	Ove Arup + Partners, London
	accoustics	Ove Arup + Partners, London
	model	Müller + Hauel, Berlin

bildnachweis / illustration credits

gsw 1	grndst	Landesbildstelle, Berlin	22
	model	Reinhard Görner, Berlin	24
	model	Charlie Stebbings, London	34
oly	model	Uwe Rau, Berlin	46
		Uwe Rau, Berlin	47
mar		Andrew Puttler, London	76
bsm	model	Uwe Rau, Berlin	93
jüd	picnic	Senatsverwaltung, Berlin	97
als	sprmd	Büro Schultes, Berlin	108
		Uwe Rau, Berlin	116
		Uwe Rau, Berlin	117
bpa	aerial view	mit freundlicher Genehmigung des Stereokat Ing. Büros, hsG Volker Zirn, Berlin	121
pho		Hans-Jürgen Wuthenow, Berlin	139
lh/ms	portrait	Charlie Stebbings, London	141